RETIR

EARLY

2 in 1

Learn How to Generate Multiple Streams of Income using
Side Hustles while Budgeting and Investing

By Christopher Kent

SIDE HUSTLE

Table of Contents

SIDE HUSTLE

Retire Early with Multiple Streams of Passive Income –
Make Money with Dropshipping, Amazon FBA,
Shopify, Affiliate Marketing, Laundromat, YouTube,
Airbnb, Blogging, etc.

By Christopher Kent

information contained within this document, including, but not limited to, — errors, omissions, or inaccuracies.

INTRODUCTION

Congratulations on purchasing the book - Side Hustle: Retire Early with Multiple Streams of Passive Income – Make Money with Dropshipping, Amazon FBA, Shopify, Affiliate Marketing, Laundromat, YouTube, Airbnb, Blogging, etc.

If you have purchased this book is it because you are ready to start claiming your financial freedom. Maybe you have read about other people doing it, or maybe you have a friend who has done it and as a result, they have an easier time paying the bills while even having some cash leftover at the end of the month. That means that not only are they able to pay their bills with greater ease but they are also able to start paying off debt faster or saving a nest egg for themselves and their family so that they no longer have to worry about finances.

In fact, many people find that they save enough that they can even start to invest it, allowing them to work less and save more. For most people, this is the ultimate goal: no longer having to work while still having passive income coming in from the various streams that they have developed over the years. Then, because of their wise money choices, they are able to start enjoying life more either by doing work that they love or by retiring altogether and spending more time with family enjoying life and traveling.

Either way, no matter what you are looking for or why adding an extra income to your life is always a great idea. In *Side Hustle,* you are going to discover nineteen different side hustles that you can add to your life so that you can start enjoying financial freedom, too. Whether you are looking for something that you can get fully engaged in or something that you can let run without you so that the income is entirely passive, you are bound to find some great ideas in this book.

Side Hustle was written to not only help you identify possible side hustles but also qualify the ones that will suit your needs and ultimately get started with the one that is going to be your next big earner. So, regardless of what you need, if you are looking for an extra $1,000+ per month, you are definitely going to discover exactly how to start.

Are you ready to dive in and find your next side hustle? If so, let's begin!

CHAPTER 1

WHY YOU NEED A SIDE HUSTLE

First things first, let's dig into why you even need a side hustle in the first place. The truth is, there are many reasons why someone would want to have a side hustle in their lives. Side hustles provide extra income that can be used for virtually anything, from travelling more to saving more money to be used toward future expenses like retirement or anything else that you feel you need to get more money going toward. Many people will use side hustles to fund multiple things at once, from debt repayment to enjoying life more on a day to day basis. Truly, there is no right or wrong way to use your side hustle money since it is all just additional money on top of what you already have available to you on a monthly basis.

Most people who have a side hustle also find that they feel more empowered because they have more than just one or two income streams coming into their household. This means that if they needed to take a day off work or even quit their job and find a new one, they would have plenty of money to help them get through that period of time. Knowing that you are not at the mercy of your boss, even if your boss is nice, can feel liberating because it begins to feel like you can make choices for yourself and that no one else can control what you choose to do with your life.

Another big reason why having a side hustle is ideal is because if you use your side hustle correctly you can actually turn that side hustle into a full-time income, even if you are building it passively. This means that if you stay committed and you keep working at it long enough you will begin to discover that your side hustle helps you completely quit your work and enjoy life solely based off of the income you are earning from that side hustle. For many people, this is the goal so they both scale the side hustle and use that income to fund and scale even more side hustles so that, in no time at all, they have plenty of money coming in from various sources funding their lifestyle. This multiple streams of income even from side hustles can be empowering because it means that if ever one does not serve as well one month you can rely on one of your others to help you pull through.

Lastly, side hustles are often started just for money but many people also tie their side hustle into something they love. What can end up happening is you start something because you need extra money but then you discover that you love what you are doing so you keep doing it. As a result, you find yourself not only making money but having a ton of fun doing it which is a huge win for most people. If you are someone who hates your day job, switching into a high paying side gig that you love can be liberating and exhilarating.

If you know that a side hustle is right for you and you are ready to start one, the next nineteen chapters are going to introduce you to excellent side hustles that you can get started with that will help you earn some extra income. Dive in, now!

CHAPTER 2

LAUNDROMAT

Although this may sound oddly specific, laundromats are actually a lucrative business opportunity that can earn you a massive income. Just think about it: all day long people are coming into a laundromat to do laundry and keep their clothes clean. Laundry machines are always needed and, if you are in an area where people tend to use laundromats often, then you can feel confident that your business will stay busy. Read on to learn more about why laundromats are such a great passive income opportunity.

Why Laundromats Work

Coin-operated laundry first started when buildings stopped putting laundry machines into their units and people had to go elsewhere to do laundry. They worked as excellent alternatives because not only did laundromats give people a place to do laundry in the first place, but they also gave people a place to do laundry quickly because people no longer had to wait for one load to be done before starting the next load. Instead, they could run several loads at once and be done their laundry far sooner.

Another reason why laundromats are such a great idea is that they do not require you to restock a store or restaurant on a regular basis, meaning that your outgoing expenses are predictable and lower than most other brick and mortar style businesses. This means that you are far more likely to earn profit with coin-operated laundry machines than you are other businesses because all of your clients are putting money right into your pocket and you are putting very little out for it.

Laundromats can be completely passive, too, if you choose to set one up and get someone else working for you. This way, your business can keep running as a complete side hustle while you go ahead and continue working at your job, allowing your laundromat to earn a passive monthly income for you.

What You Need To Get Started

What you will need to start up a laundromat business will ultimately depend on whether you want to be fully engaged with the business or have other people run it entirely. If you want other people to run it entirely it will cost you more because you will have to pay other peoples' wages, however, it also means that you can go about life as usual while your company earns you money. The average cost to start up a laundromat is about $200,000 - $500,000, which will help you acquire a building to run your business in, the machines, and all other business-related tools such as a desk for your attendant and anything else that is needed. You are also going to need to have individuals willing to work for you so that you are not attempting to run the business all on your own as this would no longer be a side hustle. As well, most laundromats are open 6 AM – 10 PM 7 days a week, which means that no one person could reasonably keep up with all of those working hours.

How To Get Started

Starting your laundromat will require you to first identify where a laundromat would be most likely to succeed so that you can purchase or lease a building that is going to be in an ideal area. Remember, people are bringing their laundry to you so they are not going to want to drive terribly far to get to your facilities. Ideally, being around residential buildings that are known for not having laundry machines built-in, such as around a lot of smaller apartments, is a great opportunity for you to put in a laundromat.

In addition to having the right place, you will also need to have the right equipment and staffing to help you get started. You are going to want to purchase as many coin-operated laundry machines as you can fit into your building, as well as other business essentials such as a desk with a chair for your staff, filing systems, and other office supplies to keep your laundromat running. You may also wish to stock small amounts of laundry supplies such as detergents and fabric softener so that people who are not prepared can purchase products from you.

Of course, you are also going to need to go through the process of hiring your staff so you should be prepared to spend at least a few weeks getting your business up and running and training everyone so that you no longer need to be involved. You will likely have to be rather hands-on for the first few months, but once your laundromat is completely running and all of your staff are trained you can go back to being hands-off, allowing the laundromat to become either completely passive or semi-passive.

How Successful You Will Be

Laundromats earn anywhere from $15,000 to $200,000 per year depending on where they are located and how much business they are getting. If you choose the right location for your business you can get people flowing through the door, you can expect to make an average revenue of about $100,00 per year. Fortunately, laundromats do not require many employees, and many do not even have any employees at all but instead simply have one person arrive in the morning to open up and turn on the machines and return at night to shut off the machines. Beyond that, they have a high quality security system that looks after the building. Because of that, operating costs are extremely low meaning that most of that revenue will be kept as profit. The average laundromat owner will keep around $40,000 per year if they make an average of $100,000 per year with their business.

How to Scale Your Business

Naturally, you want to be making closer to $200,000, as opposed to the lower $15,000 that some laundromat owners make per year. For that reason, you want to know exactly how to scale your business. The best way to scale a laundromat business is to ensure that you have the best location possible and that you advertise for your business frequently. As well, adding in extra little amenities like chairs for people to wait in or a vending machine for people to buy drinks or snacks from can make your laundromat more comfortable than others. Beyond that, franchising your business and building more chains is another great opportunity for you to scale your laundromat business so that you can start earning even more.

How Long It Will Take To See Profits

As with most brick and mortar businesses, laundromats will start seeing profits within their second or third year of business. The true amount of time it will take will depend on how successful your location is, how effective your advertising is, and how much you borrowed or invested to get your business up and running.

CHAPTER 3

PUBLISHING BOOKS

Book publishing is an excellent opportunity to earn a passive or semi-passive income. The benefit of book publishing is that, if you want to, you can develop an entire brand around your author name that can eventually be capitalized on, meaning that your side hustle can become a full blown hustle if you want it to. Say, for example, you start selling books that focus on self-help, such as specifically around topics relating to relationships. If you wanted to, then, you could develop a personal brand around relationships that allow you to give relationship advice to people in need. You could then go on to do anything you wanted, from offering products or services meant to help people in relationships. In the end, your book publishing was passive or semi-passive, earned you an income, and opened the door to many new income opportunities that you can now take advantage of.

Why Book Publishing Works

Book publishing works because at the end of the day people love reading. Mostly, people love consuming knowledge about things that are relevant to them or immersing themselves in a fantasy world that takes them away from their own stressors and lets them engage in a different reality for a while. People have been consuming large amounts of books for decades, and although the format for books has switched in a big way, books are still widely popular. Whether people are buying digital books or physical books, virtually everyone owns books and many are still being bought every single day.

Publishing books means that you can get in on that action and start earning a decent income for yourself, too. When you are publishing books it can take you some time to write them, though the income that you earn after that is passive. As well, if you do not want to write your books yourself, you can always hire a ghostwriter to write them for you. Although this may cost you more up front, having a ghostwriter can make everything a lot more passive in terms of book publishing, meaning that you will earn even more at the end of the day.

What You Need To Get Started

Getting started with writing is inexpensive and typically just takes some time or a small financial investment, depending on what way you want to go. If you want to write the book yourself, you will need $100 for a Microsoft word subscription, $25+ for a book cover, and $50+ for an advertising budget to help you advertise your book when you are ready. This means that you can start for as little as $175. If you want to get someone else to write your book for you it will be a little more costly, with full-service ghostwriters typically starting at $200 and increasing in value from there depending on the length of your book.

How To Get Started

If you want to get started with writing your own book, it is as simple as sitting down with a writing program on your computer and writing out your book. You can write your book in whatever way feels right for you and then go through and edit it later on, or you can hire a writing coach or even purchase a book that guides you through the process. Having a coach or a guide can help you get the layout of your book proper and keep you on track with writing so that you get your entire book written in virtually no time at all. If you want to work with a ghostwriting service, it is as simple as finding the writer you want to work with, letting them know what you are looking for, and paying them for your services.

How Successful You Will Be

How successful you will be will ultimately depend on how well you advertise yourself and how much of a marketing budget you have. The best way to get found as a publisher is to have high quality advertisements and a personal brand developing on social media that helps promote your book so that people have a way of finding you. Unless you are working with a professional publishing agency like Hay House or Harper Collins, you are going to have to be the one getting your book out in front of the masses, which can be costly. You can do this organically through social media and grow over time, or you can invest in a self-publishing service which allows you to receive support from professional marketers and various other tools that help you get your projects out in front of your audience.

How to Scale Your Business

Scaling your publishing business is easy: publish more books. The more that you can publish books and get them out in front of your target audience, the more you are going to have to capitalize on. Keep new books coming out as often as possible, advertise a lot, and build a personal brand so that people can locate you and start following you. Building a loyal following online is a great way to have more people already ready to buy each new book that you publish.

How Long It Will Take To See Profits

You can see profits from your book in as early as 3-6 months depending on how much you invested in the book and how well you are marketing it. After that, everything you earn will be a passive income based on your marketing budget and your growing brand.

CHAPTER 4

DROPSHIPPING

Dropshipping is a great company style where you essentially build an online shop and develop a brand for it and then allow manufacturers to run your business for you. Dropshipping manufacturers are companies who stock products and then ship them directly to your customers from their warehouse. This means that every time someone lands on your website and buys something, your company profits a percentage of that sale for earning the sale for the manufacturer in the first place.

Why Dropshipping Works

Dropshipping works because online shopping is growing massively in popularity and people love shopping online. People love the feeling of ordering something online and receiving it in the mail days later, as it provides a sense of excitement around the shopping experience. As well, since you do not have to store any products or ship anything, you get to save a lot of money which means that the majority of what you earn is profit. In fact, dropshipping businesses are so easy to run that they are essentially a form of passive income, aside from the marketing that you have to do. If you hire a marketing agency to grow your brand for you online, then your dropshipping business will be completely passive.

What You Need To Get Started

To get started with a dropshipping business you are first going to need to find one or two dropshipping companies that you can work with so that you already have products available for you to stock online. Then, you are going to have to get a website developer to design your website for you unless you are already capable of designing your own websites. After that, you are going to need to have a marketing agency who can help you build a brand for and promote your dropshipping company, or at least have a budget for paid advertisements. Ultimately, anything that you are willing to do yourself can save you money, but every element of the dropshipping business can also be outsourced which means that you do not have to do anything. Because of the versatility, starting a dropshipping company can run you anywhere from $500-$10,000+.

How To Get Started

To get started, you first need to determine how much you can or how much you are willing to do on your own. Then, once you know, you can go ahead and start making the necessary connections to get your business going. If you have decided that you want this to be entirely passive and you do not want to do anything then you are going to need to find a dropshipping company to connect with, hire a website developer, hire a marketing agency, and start some basic social media accounts for your brand to be grown on. Once everything is set in place all you have to do is reinvest some of your profits into your marketing agency so that they can continue growing your brand for you. Otherwise, you just sit back and collect your profits at the end of each month.

How Successful You Will Be

Dropshipping can be incredibly successful, or a total flop depending on how well you market your business. The most successful dropshipping companies have great brands online and also have attractive and high quality shopping websites that feel similar to the websites of any other high quality store. Poor quality one-page designs with all of the products lopped onto one page often look like a scam to people so they generally do not do very well. So, if you design your page effectively and your market well, you could be profiting $500-$1000+ per month from a well-designed dropshipping company.

How to Scale Your Business

You can scale a dropshipping business in two different ways: by stocking your store with more products, or by copying your business model and starting additional dropshipping companies that cater to different product niches. If you choose to add more products to your business it will be less expensive, though if you have a successful dropshipping company already and you replicate it, it may be more profitable. You have to decide what way you want to go and how much increased profits you want to see for yourself.

How Long It Will Take To See Profits

With a dropshipping company, it can take about 6-12 months to see your profits. Although you will likely be making money within the first two months, it can take some additional time to break even on side hustles with higher startup investments. If you are not seeing profits in 12 months, you may need to redesign your business or consider switching to something you would be more effective at.

CHAPTER 5

AMAZON FBA

Amazon FBA is similar to dropshipping, except that you will need to be more involved with this business model. If you want to start with Amazon FBA, you are going to need to find the products you want to sell, purchase them from merchants, and have them shipped to Amazon's warehouses. Aside from that, however, nearly everything runs similarly to dropshipping business.

Why Amazon FBA Works

Amazon FBA is a powerful business tool because it allows you to tap into Amazon's built-in marketing program and get everything that you need to sell your products. On Amazon, you have a built-in store, built-in marketing software, and hundreds of thousands of existing customers who are already turning to Amazon to browse the platform to find products just like yours. Plus, you can make Amazon extremely passive by simply having to check in every two to four weeks to ensure that you have enough stock available for your customers. Otherwise, as long as you have a decent marketing budget behind you, you can promote your products easily and remain entirely hands-off.

What You Need To Get Started

Getting started with Amazon FBA is extremely simple. All you need to do is open up an Amazon FBA account, find a manufacturer that you can buy your products from, and get your products shipped to Amazon. Aside from that, you can set up ongoing advertisements with Amazon's marketing software so that your products just keep getting boosted up in people's feeds. They also get seen elsewhere online such as on blogs and on social media, which means that your products will get seen by a massive audience. With these tools in place, you are ready to get started. Getting started with Amazon FBA can be done with as little as $750.

How To Get Started

Once you have a merchant account and an Amazon FBA account with Amazon, all you need to do is have products shipped to Amazon's FBA warehouses. That's it.

How Successful You Will Be

Your Amazon FBA business can be incredibly successful as long as you are willing to invest a fair amount into your initial marketing budget. After you have invested your startup marketing expenses of a couple of hundred dollars, you can expect to sell plenty of products and earn your marketing expenses back and then some in no time at all. Once you have everything up and running you can make anywhere from

$1,000 to $10,000+ per month from your Amazon FBA business.

How to Scale Your Business

Scaling your Amazon FBA business is really easy: you simply find more products that you can add to your shop and then you go ahead and you start stocking them. As long as you can afford the manufacturer's fee and you can get them to your Amazon FBA warehouse, your business can expand. The key to massive expansion is to start looking for products that are low cost to acquire and that have a strong profit margin. For example, jewelry can be bought for as little as $1.00 a piece and can be sold for upward of $10 a piece. This is a massive profit margin where you are earning 10x your investment on every piece. Focusing on these types of products will help you scale fast, meaning that you will earn closer to the $10,000+ per month range as long as you scale effectively and in niches where the products are actually desirable.

How Long It Will Take To See Profits

With Amazon FBA, how long it will take for you to see your profits depends on how much stock you buy in the first place. If you buy a lot of stock early on and invest a fair bit into your marketing it could take you a bit longer to see your profits back simply because of how much you have invested. That being said, most people find that they break even and begin to see profits in as little as 3-5 months, assuming that they have entered the business with a strong marketing plan and products that were high in demand.

CHAPTER 6

SHOPIFY BUSINESSES

Shopify businesses are another form of online business that you can run that can help you earn a fair amount of money online. If you run a Shopify business, you can build your own personal brand and have the products in your store branded for you or your company as well. This is a fun way to build an online business with an existing backend platform that allows you to stand out. If you want to make a splash in the world of online retail, Shopify can be a great place to start.

Why Shopify Businesses Work

Shopify gives you the unique advantage of not being up against thousands of other merchants as you would be on a platform like Amazon. Although Shopify has many different businesses running through it, it is also running each business independently with its own store front and web address. This means that people go to a unique domain name to find your store which is not linked to a bigger merchant, like Amazon. The one drawback with a store like this is that you do have to do a lot more marketing for yourself as you do not have existing traffic already eligible to find your products. Instead, you have to make traffic to your domain name for yourself, which can take some time and practice.

What You Need To Get Started

Getting started with Shopify is as easy as opening up an account, sourcing products to sell, purchasing those products, and then launching your business. If you do not want to sell physical products you can always sell digital products which can actually earn you a higher profit because they are cheaper to make and they do not require you to ship anything to your client. Once you have your shop and products available, you are also going to need to go ahead and open up some social media accounts and start branding your business. If you have never branded a business before there are plenty of great guides online, or you might consider getting started with a branding coach or a marketing company who can help you. All that to be considered, starting a Shopify store can cost you anywhere from $750 - $4,000.

How To Get Started

Getting started with your Shopify store is easy. First, you need to decide what brand you want to develop and what niche of products you want to be selling. Since this is all housed under one brand and one store, you want to make sure that all of your products fit into the same niche. Once you have discovered your ideal niche, you need to name your store and start developing a brand for it on social media. You also want to start looking for merchants who sell products that are relevant to your brand so that you can start acquiring products to sell. Ideally, you should have at least 5-10 products in your store to get started so that you are not attempting to market a store with 1-2 items to people. The more products you have to get started with, the better. If you can, consider buying 5-10 of each unique item and then buying a wider range of items so that you can have more variety in your store. This will also allow you to get a better idea of what people are buying from you so that you can stock more of what your audience wants and less of what they do not want.

How Successful You Will Be

Shopify businesses can be wildly successful, earning you $500 - $1000+ per month, with many people regularly making over $5,000 - $10,000 per month with their shop. The big key with Shopify is that you want to make sure that you are effectively marketing your shop so that people can actually find it. If you are not regularly sharing your shop with people and introducing them to what you have available then you are not getting the opportunity to even show them your shop. Having a strong brand online makes all of the difference, as your social media platforms and paid advertisements are how you are going to funnel people to your website. The more people that land there, the better. Because of the necessity of the brand, Shopify can be an income stream that needs quite a bit of your work and involvement to work. However, you can also consider hiring a marketing agency to look after everything so that it is all done for you and you do not have to do anything to get your products in front of other people.

How to Scale Your Business

Scaling your Shopify business comes from scaling your brand and adding more products. As with other online retail shops, the more products that you can stock with larger profit margins, the more you are going to earn. A big way that many Shopify store owners scale their business is by expanding their niche, or by offering highly trending products that people are actively looking for. If you can get your hands on trending products and price them slightly under the average market value, not only will you have something that everyone wants but you will also have one of the best prices. This is a great way to get a massive amount of eyes turned onto your business, fast.

How Long It Will Take To See Profits

With Shopify, it can take closer to 6 months or even a year before you see profits as there is quite a bit that goes into getting a Shopify store profitable. Understand that your profit is heavily reliant on people actually being able to find your store in the first place, as well as them being able to have confidence in the products that you are offering and your brand in general. Most successful brands that are earning large amounts of money have done a lot to earn people's trust, which has resulted in people feeling confident buying from them. Unless you already have a brand, you need to expect to spend some time establishing that trust so that people feel confident buying from you, too. Once you have developed that trust, your profits should start showing up and growing rapidly.

CHAPTER 7

TUTORING

Tutoring is a surprisingly great way to make extra money on the side, although it will take some of your time. Depending on how you do it, tutoring could require all hands on deck, or it could be a semi-passive income stream that you develop to earn money from. If you become a tutor yourself, you are going to be working all the time to earn your money. If, however, you choose to hire other tutors and you simply focus on bringing in clients for those tutors, it can be passive as all you need to do is screen your tutors and market to acquire clients. For this chapter, we are going to talk about what you can do if you are the tutor, and how you can grow your tutoring business.

Why Tutoring Works

Many people want to hire support for themselves or their children to learn about their studies with greater confidence. Learning in classes can be challenging, and sometimes ineffective because there simply is not enough time and attention for lessons to be absorbed and for personal questions to be asked. For that reason, a tutor is a great opportunity for people to get access to that 1:1 help that they may need to help them consume all of the necessary information and feel confident in knowing it. Tutors are always being hired and regularly make $10-$25 per hour in the United States, depending on what you are tutoring on. For example, a tutor for a 5th grade math student will likely earn less than a tutor for a college medical student. Still, many people regularly need help with their studies and you may be able to offer that help by being their tutor.

What You Need To Get Started

Getting started as a tutor is simple and extremely inexpensive. Generally, you can start by having a strong educational background and a few strong connections in your community. You may not even need to do any marketing if you already know of enough people who would benefit from your services, or who could connect you to people who could. For that reason, all you need is a strong network and a solid educational background to get started. You can often start working as a tutor for as little as $0. Even though it is 2019, many people still market their tutoring services on a simple flier smartly placed somewhere locally.

How To Get Started

Getting started as a tutor is simple: connect with someone in your network and get started working with a student! Chances are you are going to need to go through an interview process so that whoever you will be working for knows that you are qualified to educate them on what you are teaching. Your interview will generally be an opportunity for you to introduce yourself, your skills, and your prices so that people know what they can expect from you and if you are the right fit. If you do not know how to price yourself, you can look at other tutors in your area and price yourself accordingly. Alternatively, you might consider looking at a local tutoring agency and get hired through them. For this, you will likely require proof that you are as educated as you say you are, that you are capable of teaching this knowledge, and a criminal record check to ensure that the agency feels confident sending you into their clients' homes. If you work this way, your wage will likely be determined for you by the agency.

How Successful You Will Be

Tutors make an average of $17.50 per hour in the United States, which means that you could be earning around $700 - $1,500 or more per month depending on how much time you are willing to invest in this side hustle. Obviously, the more time you invest the more you are going to earn since tutoring is done on an hourly basis. Most tutors are highly successful, especially if they spend time developing networks in communities of either parents of school aged children or people who are in post-secondary educational programs. The bigger your network, the more likely you are going to be recommended to paying clients so that you can begin working with even more people.

How to Scale Your Business

Scaling your tutoring business can be done either by working more hours or by turning your business into an agency. If you have more clients than you can handle yourself you can always consider turning your business into an agency by hiring other tutors who are qualified to help teach people and earning a percentage of their wages. Then, all you have to do is assign them to your network of people and have them teaching for you. This way, you earn your own wages as well as a percentage of the wages of the tutors that you represent. If you do this, it is important that you set your agency up like an agency and look into your local laws to ensure that you are working within your legal obligations. For example, many agencies like this need to require criminal record checks from their tutors so that they can guarantee that they are not sending criminals into peoples' homes. After all, things like that could come back on you as a liability since you are representing that person through your agency.

How Long It Will Take To See Profits

With tutoring, since it is a $0 start up you can begin seeing profits immediately. Most tutors will require their clients to pay per session, so right from your very first session with a client, you will be earning money. This means that you can start seeing your $1,000+ per month profits in as little as one month as long as you get yourself enough clients working with you.

CHAPTER 8

BLOGGING

Blogging exists in nearly every recommended side hustle list and that is because it works. Many people have argued that blogging is "dead" or that no one reads blogs anymore because they have become so washed out from too many people doing it, but the truth is that blogs are still very much relevant and people are still making $1,000 - $10,000+ per month off of their blogs. If you want to get in on the action, starting your own blog is a great opportunity to have a passion project that earns you big bucks.

Why Blogging Works

Blogging works because people love learning about other people's opinions and reading about other people's lives. Think about it: how many times have you Googled something to discover the answer that you needed? Whether you wanted to know about the latest celebrity buzz or a great recipe that you could cook for under $5, chances are the Google result that you landed on was none other than a blog. Blogs continue to provide high amounts of information for people who are searching for content on the internet. Assuming that you utilize effective SEO measures and talk about something relevant, you can be the one that comes up when people search for a certain subject. As a result, your page grows in popularity which means that money making features like advertisements and sponsored posts begin to earn you a higher income, thus making your blog profitable. Because you are required to write posts for your blog and continue promoting it, blogging is considered to be a semi-passive income stream, although you could make it more passive by hiring writers to write for you if you wanted.

What You Need To Get Started

Getting started with a blog is extremely simple: you can generally start for less than $100 by finding a hosting platform and purchasing a period of hosting time as well as a domain name. Once you have that in place all you have to do is design your blog and begin uploading posts. If you use a platform like Squarespace or Wix, creating your blog is simple as these are click-and-build platforms that allow you to create beautiful websites for inexpensive. Alternatively, if you are more tech savvy or you feel like paying $1,000+ for a website, you can always hire someone to help you create a WordPress website which is typically more customizable but can be significantly more challenging to set up.

How To Get Started

Getting started with your blogging is simple. After you have everything set up, you will want to pick a niche that is relevant to both you and your target audience so that you feel comfortable writing about the topic and people are actually interested in reading about it. If you have never had to pick a niche before, consider looking into something that interests you and then exploring niches related to that subject. You want to choose a niche that has a steady audience that regularly consumes new content to avoid trying to market so hard to a less active audience that will be harder to reach. After you have picked your niche you will want to write 10-15 starter posts for your blog so that you can promote it and give your readers a healthy amount of content to begin reading right away. Then, you want to have a posting schedule so that you are regularly uploading new content on a consistent basis, thus keeping people coming back to your page. Other than that, consistently sharing your content to social media platforms and encouraging people to share the content that they resonate with is the best way to keep your content being seen by your audience.

How Successful You Will Be

A large number of people find great success in blogging for profit, and find that they are earning $200+ per month in the first three months of their blogging career. After that, profits will generally steadily increase until you are earning $1,000+ per month within 6-12 months, depending on how you approach your blog. The big key here is that you need to be uploading and marketing your blog consistently, as this is how you are going to build your reputation and gain credibility. If you do not take the time to consistently get your name out there and show people that you are blogging, chances are you are going to lose credibility fast and therefore your advertisements and sponsored posts will be less valuable. If you want to grow value, you have to build your reputation up and get your audience seeing how trustworthy you are.

How to Scale Your Business

Scaling your blogging business will ultimately come from establishing and developing your blogging reputation, as your blog becomes more valuable the more traffic that you gain on a consistent basis. As you continue to receive increasing amounts of traffic on your blog, you can begin to promote this as being your success point, which makes you valuable to potential advertisers who want to promote with blogs like yours. So, as long as you continue increasing your value by sharing great and relevant content and promoting it effectively, your blog will grow.

Another great way to grow your blog is to consider spreading beyond your blog. Many bloggers will also establish their presence on social media so that when they are promoting their blog they are also growing their influencer accounts. This is especially common on Instagram where being an influencer can be especially valuable because you can profit from Instagram itself, too. This way, you can be earning money from sponsored social media posts *and* your blog, meaning that your entire brand expands, you become even more valuable, and your posts earn even more money for you. People who do this effectively can earn upward of $5,000 - $10,000+ per month from their blogs.

How Long It Will Take To See Profits

With blogging, your time to profitability naturally depends on how much you have invested and how much you are investing time wisely. If you start off smaller and invest consistent time every single day to writing for your blog and promoting it to other people, chances are you will start seeing a fairly consistent profit within 3-6 months, and that profit will continue steadily growing as you continue blogging.

CHAPTER 9

AFFILIATE MARKETING

Affiliate marketing is a great tool that you can use when it comes to creating a side hustle. If you already have a network established, affiliate marketing can begin earning you an income right away. Alternatively, you can develop a social media presence, a steady blog, or both and begin using this as a way to develop an audience to market to. Effectively building up an audience who is readily consuming your content is a great opportunity to ensure that you have plenty of people to market products to, which makes you a valuable asset to many different companies.

Why Affiliate Marketing Works

Affiliate marketing works by having you market products for companies to your already established audience. Many people find that their well-established audiences are readily willing to consume anything they offer because they feel confident that what that person markets is going to be positive and useful. As a result, any time their audience purchases something through their affiliate link, the affiliate is paid for a percentage of that income. Affiliate marketing works because consumers prefer word of mouth and social proof to prove that the products they are investing in are actually worth their investment. When people see that many other individuals are also having a positive experience with a brand, they are more likely to develop an interest in that brand and want to try it out for themselves. Even products that someone would normally never purchase will be purchased by an individual if someone they trust is excited enough about the products and swears by them. This is why so many "as seen on TV" products become fads: we see people on TV promoting them, one of our friends gives them a shot, and then suddenly everyone has them. Remember Eggies, Snuggies, and Sham Wows? All of these products blew up because of social proof, and the people who were affiliated with these products made a ton of money promoting them.

What You Need To Get Started

Getting started as an affiliate marketer is rather simple: you just need to have a strong network of people who trust in you to market your products to so that they are more likely to want to buy from you. You can get started with affiliate marketing by developing this network if you do not already have one so that you have an audience to market to, thus meaning that anyone willing to put in this legwork can get started. Most people who get involved in affiliate marketing will develop a strong online presence with their audience through Instagram, Facebook, Twitter, YouTube, or blogging. This way, they have a consistent platform to reach people and, because it is developed online, they can easily reach people who would have otherwise been impossible for them to reach through in person efforts. Once you have a trusting audience who is consistently engaging with your content you can go ahead and begin finding companies with affiliate programs that you can sign up with so that you can start marketing to your audience!

How To Get Started

After you have developed your strong network, all you need to do to get started with affiliate marketing is to find companies who have affiliate programs and who sell products relevant to you and your audience. Then, you sign up for these programs and receive a special link or code that your followers can use to purchase products through. Once you have those links, all you have to do is go ahead and start promoting their products to your audience. You want to make sure that all of your promotional posts are well-written and sound like you so that even though people know you are marketing to them it still feels authentic and genuine. Anything that does not sound like you will sound fake and may diminish your credibility online. Make sure that you always look at the rules on any platform that you are using, as well as for your locale, as many platforms and states have rules around how you can engage in affiliate marketing. It is important that you follow these rules so that your business stays legitimate and you can continue marketing to your audience and earning money this way for a long time.

How Successful You Will Be

Most affiliate marketers who place a strong emphasis on developing an audience and establishing credibility with their audience will earn upward of $2,500+ per month, with many falling in the $5,000 - $10,000+ range. If you want to establish credibility and really generate success you are going to always want to place your focus on developing an audience who trusts you and who likes you. This is typically done by having an audience who you continually work toward building a friendship with by regularly sharing your life with them and letting them see who you really are. The more you show that you are an authentic person, the more people will relate to you and the more they are going to want to trust in you and purchase what you share with them.

How to Scale Your Business

Scaling your affiliate marketing business will work much in the same way as scaling a blogging business. You can scale your affiliate marketing business by continually growing your audience and driving more traffic to your affiliate marketing links. When it comes to your affiliate marketing business, your value is perceived by the number of followers you have on social media and how engaged your followers are. Ideally, someone with a large audience that is also largely engaged is someone who is going to have more traffic coming through to their page, making them a more valuable asset. This way, if you choose to start an affiliate deal with someone, you know that you have enough people engaging with you that you should make a decent profit off of the deal. Likewise, the larger your audience grows and the more engaged they are, the more likely brands are going to start reaching out to you and promoting to you because they want to reach your audience. This means that the more time you spend refining your audience and growing it steadily, the more valuable you become and the more profits you are going to earn.

How Long It Will Take To See Profits

Because it is free to develop a network and grow your social media account, you can begin seeing profits in your affiliate marketing business right from your very first deal. The consistent profits will generally start rolling in between 3-6 months after you begin your affiliate marketing business and, for most, they will consistently reach above $1,000 per month within the first year of business. Of course, as with anything of this nature, the more you are committed to building your presence and developing trust with your audience, the more you are going to be growing online. This means that your credibility and value go up and your earnings will also go up. So, the more you focus on credibility and trust, the sooner you will see significant profits.

CHAPTER 10

MULTI-LEVEL MARKETING

Contrary to popular belief, multi-level marketing, and affiliate marketing are not one in the same. Although the work itself is the same, since you are promoting products to your network, multi-level marketing actually has the capacity to earn you a greater income because you are not putting so much work into keeping your audience growing. With multi-level marketing, there are far more ways to earn income and there are also opportunities for you to earn residual income that comes in each month regardless of whether or not you post anything. For that reason, getting into multi-level marketing may be more desirable to some people. However, multi-level marketing does come with the reputation of being a scam or something not worthy of peoples' investments, so you may have to put some work in getting beyond this belief system as you start developing your business.

Why Multi-Level Marketing Works

Multi-level marketing works because it provides you with the opportunity to grow a network that you profit off of, essentially. With multi-level marketing, you earn an income both from your customers who purchase from you and from people who join to sell products with you. If you build your network effectively, you could be earning upward of $100,000 per month from multi-level marketing. In fact, multi-level marketing has been said to create more millionaires than any other industry in the world. Multi-level marketing works because there are so many ways that you earn income from your business, and many of those ways are consistently earning for you even when you are not putting any work in. For example, if you grow a network of people who are running their businesses after recruiting through you, also known as a "down line," you can earn a percentage of their income, too. This is how many people become millionaires through this business model and retire without even having to work their multi-level marketing business anymore.

What You Need To Get Started

Multi-level marketing is a semi-passive business opportunity that can become completely passive if you work it enough in the beginning. In order to get started, all you need is a network of people that you can market to, which can easily be grown online if you want to have a larger reach within your audience. Then, you also need a company that you can join, someone who can recruit you, and a team who is going to help you achieve success. Other than that, you will need anywhere from $50 - $2,500 to purchase the starter kit for your company so that you can sign up as a marketer and have products that you can start promoting to your audience. Ideally, if you have never tried the company before you will purchase some basic products from your potential sponsor first so that you can give them a try and honestly endorse them to your audience.

How To Get Started

To get started with multi-level marketing, you have to consider what business is going to be most relevant to you and what you are going to get the most use out of. Finding the right industry that fits in with your lifestyle is a great opportunity to make sure that you are getting everything you want and need out of your company. It also ensures that it is easy for you to market the products because you are already likely to be using them on a regular basis in your life anyway, so now you are just swapping them out, promoting them, and earning an income from that. Once you have considered an industry that makes sense to you, you can go ahead and find a company that has a compensation plan that is going to earn you big profits. You want to have a company with a compensation plan that is easy to understand and that earns you plenty so that you can start earning money as soon as possible, and so that you can easily explain to other people how the earnings work, too. After you have found your company, you want to sign up with the biggest kit that you can afford and then go ahead and start marketing the products out of your starter kit!

How Successful You Will Be

Developing success with a multi-level marketing company all comes down to your mindset, which unfortunately is the failing point for many people. If you have a poor mindset where you already believe that multi-level marketing is a scam and that you are ripping people off or that you are not going to make money because "no one ever does," naturally you are not going to make any money with this opportunity. However, if you can surround yourself with positive and inspiring people and start focusing on how great the opportunity is and how people are already succeeding with it, you can generate massive success. The difference between the people who quit and the people who make $100,000+ per month is that the ones who make millions of dollars per year refused to listen to the crowd and went ahead anyway. As a result, they generated massive success and found themselves living as millionaires early on.

How to Scale Your Business

The key to scaling a multi-level marketing business is to keep talking about your company with people and offering it to people who might be interested. Make it easy for people to join you, show them how much fun you are having and how big your profits are, and have confidence in sharing your products. Show those people that this is going to be your opportunity to grow and that you are making plenty of money off of your business, regardless of what anyone is saying about you or your company. As your team starts to grow, put in the effort to educate them on how to market effectively and pass around high quality marketing skills that set you and your team apart from the crowd. The more you and your team grow beyond the status quo for the multi-level marketing industry, the more success you are going to have with your business.

How Long It Will Take To See Profits

Understanding the timeline for seeing profits with multi-level marketing can be tricky because it varies greatly. On one hand, you could sign up with a company for very little and start earning profits rapidly *if* you were consistently getting sales. However, most smaller business kits do not have the capacity to earn as many sales because you do not have as many products to show people and people do not take you quite as seriously. On the other hand, if you buy a $2,500+ kit you may take a while to see profits back because of the amount of your initial investment. However, people do realize that you are way more serious about it and that you must be in love with the products if you purchased that many. For that reason, your sweet spot for making fast profits likely lies in the medium range of $250-$1,000 starter kits. However, if you want to accumulate a larger amount of profits over time, you may be better to buy a kit in the $750-$2,500 range. The standard time period to start seeing consistent profits for a multi-level marketing company is 9-18 months, and it typically takes around 2-3 years to start earning over $50,000+ per month.

CHAPTER 11

YOUTUBE

YouTube is a great social media platform that can earn you a significant amount of profits if you leverage the platform correctly. Like blogging, YouTube has many ways for you to earn an income and it can be done by having a consistent stream of people watching your page. The more you spend time building your YouTube channel, the more income you are going to earn this way, so know that this can be a very lucrative income opportunity if you let it be. Believe it or not, YouTube was the original platform for influencers, and it still has a strong capacity to help people establish themselves as influencers on the internet. For that reason, it is a strong platform for people to start using if they want to earn a side income doing something fun and enjoyable.

Why YouTube Works

If you enjoy developing videos and speaking in front of a camera, YouTube can be an incredible business opportunity. Getting on YouTube and sharing videos about what you are doing or products that you are loving is a great opportunity for you to begin creating a presence for yourself and establishing credibility and trust with your audience. When people see you on camera, they have a greater likelihood of trusting in you because they feel as though you are talking directly to them, which helps them feel like you are being more personable and friendly. For many, this activates the part of their mind that feels connected to another human, making it easier for them to believe in you and in what you are saying. This is exactly why video marketing is taking off and so many people are seeing increased benefit from video marketing over any other marketing method. Once you have established this credible presence, you can make money on YouTube through monetizing your channel with advertisements, sharing sponsored videos, and promoting affiliate marketing products in your videos.

What You Need To Get Started

Getting started with YouTube can be a little more costly as you need to make sure that you have all of the right things to help you get started. If you want to get started as cheap as possible you can find a high quality camera within your budget, and maybe a tripod to prop your camera on. If you get started this way, your YouTube channel can cost as little as $600 to get started. It is important to make sure that you buy a camera that shoots in at least 1080p, however, as anything lower and your audience is not going to want to watch your videos. If you want to get started a little more high end and have a great channel from the start, you can purchase a nicer camera, a tripod, a ring light, and decent editing software like iMovie or Final Cut Pro, each of which is a great tool to use. These tools can cost you around $1,250 to get started, however, they will not need to be replaced or upgraded as soon so you can likely get away with these tools for much longer than you could a cheap camera and a cheap tripod. Either way, however, start with what fits your budget and go from there.

How To Get Started

Getting started on YouTube ultimately comes with making videos that are interesting and relevant and that show you off to your audience. You can use your expertise in a certain niche industry to educate your audience on various things or, if you would prefer, you can use your knack for comedy to make videos that are entertaining and interesting to your audience. Once you know the content that you want to create, all you have to do is set up your equipment and start filming. Then, afterward, you can edit your video and upload it to a YouTube channel. Ideally, you should create a YouTube channel that has a relevant name, attractive channel art, a profile picture, and a description that helps people know what you are all about. If you want to take your platform next level you can also include a channel trailer that welcomes people to your page as soon as they find it on desktop.

How Successful You Will Be

YouTube success depends on your ability to create high quality videos that are relevant while also being able to market them effectively to an audience who is going to watch your videos. If you get all three of these parts of your YouTube channel sorted out you can become highly successful, with many popular YouTube channels earning upward of $5,000 per month in their first two years in business. In your first year, you can expect to start earning upward of $1,000 per month in your first six months if you treat your channel as a business and not just a place to share videos. A great way to set yourself up for success is to follow other successful YouTube creators in your niche, and others in general, and do what you can to replicate what they are doing in terms of how they are creating and marketing content. The more clear you are with your marketing, the more effective your channel will grow and therefore the more you will stand to earn.

How to Scale Your Business

The best way to scale your YouTube business is to set yourself up for success right from the start. Choose a niche that has plenty of opportunities for you to promote as an affiliate, share sponsored videos, and get paid content out there. The more expandable your niche is, the more you are going to be able to grow into it and start taking advantage of all of the niche's opportunities because you will have set yourself up for success from day one. Once you have found that niche and started growing in it, all you need to do is go ahead and keep building up your audience so that you can increase your channel's traffic. Remember the more people who watch your videos, the more people that you have to market to which means that you also have a greater chance of earning a higher profit from your channel.

How Long It Will Take To See Profits

With YouTube, it can take a significant period of time to see profits if you are not fully educated in what you are doing. If you start your channel off poorly and do not begin by creating high quality videos with a clear purpose right from the start, you are going to find yourself taking 6-12 months or even longer to consistently make a profit off of your channel. If, however, you pretend that you are already wildly successful and you start making the highest quality videos that you can from day 1 and you promote them regularly, you can start earning a higher profit sooner. Some YouTube creators report having earned their profit in as early as month 3, and with a consistent profit rolling in by month 6. The more consistent that you can be with creating high quality content for your audience, the sooner you will begin seeing your profitable income.

CHAPTER 12

TURO

Turo is a car rental company whereby people who own their cars can rent their cars out to individuals who need a temporary car and earn money from it. This is an excellent opportunity for anyone who owns their own car and does not use it on a regular basis to rent out their car and receive extra income from that. Many people are using it as a way to earn an extra income on their secondary cars, or for people who are interested in renting out their primary car if they are not using it often to earn a profit, too.

Why Turo Works

Turo works because people are always interested in renting cars and, for the most part, renting from a person is cheaper and easier than renting from a business. Not only is it easier to get approved to rent these cars, but it is also easier for the payment, pick up, and drop off to be handled because it is being dealt with directly through the owner, and Turo. As a car owner, Turo works because you are being protected by a company who ensures that you and your vehicle are protected. This also means that you do not have to advertise your car for rent as you can simply put it on Turo and let their search engine based market place do the work for you. As a result, all you have to do is get your car on there and start earning bookings, which will earn you a profit from your vehicle.

What You Need To Get Started

Getting started with Turo is easy, all you need is a vehicle that you own and that has the right insurance for you to be using it as a rental car. Then, you can create a Turo account and upload your car with any information that is relevant to your car so that people can decide whether or not they want to rent it. After that, you simply wait for the rental offers to start coming in! If you have offered to drop off and pick up the car you will also need to have a plan in place to arrange this so that you can have your car delivered and received from the renter. Other than these few basic startup requirements, you can go ahead and start renting your car on Turo!

How To Get Started

Before you start renting out your car it is important that you talk to your insurance company and get the proper insurance on your car for business use. Not having the right insurance on your car can cause Turo to deny your car being able to be rented out, and it can cause serious liabilities for you if someone rents out your car and gets into an accident or otherwise causes trouble with it. In some cases, it can cause your insurer to deny you insurance in the future because they now see you as high risk and they do not want to offer you insurance. Once you have the right insurance on, you will need to go to Turo's website and set up an account as someone who owns a vehicle that they are ready to rent out. From there, Turo will walk you through the process of setting up your account and getting your car listed on their platform. They will also ensure that you know of any guidelines or requirements as a vehicle owner to be working with them, and it is important that you pay attention. Remember, this is a business and you are renting out your car so you want to be professional and thorough about the entire process to ensure that you earn a profit without accidentally running into liability issues due to a lack of thoroughness.

How Successful You Will Be

Depending on how often your car is available and how much you are able to charge per day, you can easily start earning $1,000+ per month on Turo. Your maximum earnable income on this platform will ultimately depend on how nice your car is, how well priced it is compared to other similar vehicles, and how frequently you can keep your vehicle rented out for. The more your vehicle is rented, obviously, the more you will earn money from this service.

How to Scale Your Business

Scaling your Turo business can either be done by making your car more readily available or purchasing and renting out a second car if you find that you are earning enough to make this a wise move. Not everyone will find that this makes sense for them, however, so for many people, they simply earn an additional income off of their car and that is it. Still, if you wanted to, you could go ahead and start purchasing nicer cars and renting them out consistently to earn a profit. It all depends on how much you are making per month and if it seems feasible to purchase another car or not.

How Long It Will Take To See Profits

With Turo, you can begin seeing profits as early as your first month, so long as your car gets rented out. Since most cars have fairly consistent rental rates, you can expect to be seeing your $1,000+ income from Turo in as little as 3-6 months, as long as you keep your car readily available and keep your ratings up. At the end of each rental period, the renter has the opportunity to rate you and your car and if these ratings stay high your car is more likely to be rented out. If, however, these ratings go down, you may make it hard to get your car rented out again which can mean that you are going to lose your opportunity to earn a profit from Turo.

CHAPTER 13

AIRBNB

Airbnb is like Turo except for homes. Many people who have vacation homes, or who have larger homes where they can afford to rent out a room or a private suite in their home use Airbnb as an opportunity to earn money from their home. Keeping your home rented out this way is a great opportunity to start earning an income on space that you are not using without having to have it permanently rented out. Many property owners prefer this because they can simply make the property unavailable to be rented any time they want to use the property and they can rent it out anytime they are not using the property for an income. This makes the property more flexible because it can be used by both the home owner and vacationers, rather than having it permanently rented out and unavailable to be used by the home owner.

Why Airbnb Works

Airbnb works because people are always looking for a place to stay when they are travelling and for many staying in an Airbnb feels way more personable and comfortable than staying in a hotel. Hotels can be very cold and unwelcoming and while they have room service and built-in amenities like pools and gyms, they can also be uncomfortable. Often, the rooms are small, the bathrooms are not too nice, and they can feel cramped. Airbnb vacation homes, however, can feel far more comfortable and accommodating because they are true homes. Most times, the owner decorates it like a home and it feels comfortable and cozy and far more accommodating for guests. Many Airbnb properties also have direct access to outside which means that they can be enjoyed by people who are not interested in being cramped in tiny rooms with very little space to do anything. Because of how comfortable they can be, Airbnb can be a great opportunity for vacationers to feel more at ease during their travels, which means that home owners have a great opportunity to rent to these interested vacationers.

What You Need To Get Started

In order to get started with Airbnb, you are going to need to have a property that you can rent out and permission to rent out part of your property if you are not the direct owner of that property. Not every land owner will be okay with their renters renting out parts of the property to vacationers, so make sure that you get an agreement in writing if your land owner says it is okay to avoid legal troubles in the future. Otherwise, if you are a land owner yourself then you are in the clear. However, you may need to check your local bylaws as not all locales allow Airbnb type rentals due to poor economies or housing crisis for people who already live in the area. As long as you are legally in the clear, you can go ahead and upgrade your home insurance to accommodate for Airbnb renters and then begin renting out your property!

How To Get Started

To get started with Airbnb you are going to need to create an account on Airbnb that is designed for property owners. Your profile is going to require you to have your own personal profile that will be attached to your rentals, as this is how Airbnb promotes each property: by also promoting the property owner. This gives each property a more personal feel, as well as gives renters an idea of who they will be renting from so that they feel more comfortable with staying with you or on your property. After making your personal profile, you will go ahead and make a listing for each of the properties that you have available to be rented. Each property will need a name, a description, high quality photographs, and information about how it can be rented and what the rules are for anyone who stays on your property. Once all of this is set up, all you have to do is leave your listing up and let Airbnb promote your property in searches until someone decides to rent your property from them!

How Successful You Will Be

Airbnb has been known to help people make a massive amount of income off of their property. The thing about Airbnb is that profits can shift from month to month as seasons shift and travelers are either visiting frequently or not as much because the traveling season is over. That being said, if you can get a nice property that is well-priced and enjoyable to stay at, you could earn as much as $10,000 per month during peak season. Despite the months fluctuating, Airbnb is known for having nearly 50% of all of their hosts earning more than $500 per month, which makes it an excellent platform for you to get on and earn money with.

How to Scale Your Business

Scaling your Airbnb business will work if you either purchase more property to rent or you have more space that you can make available. Alternatively, increasing your amount of availability and keeping your host rating high so that people know that you are a great place to stay at is another way that you can scale your business. The more people know about you and see you as having the best property with the best experience, the more people are going to want to stay with you, which will keep you booked up more frequently. This way, if having more property or more time availability is not feasible, then at least you are maximizing what you already have and earning as much as you can off of your property.

How Long It Will Take To See Profits

With Airbnb, the platform itself dramatically reduces the amount of time it takes to see rental profits from vacation properties. It also reduces the amount of time that it takes to make your money back since you are not renting per month but instead per night, which means that you are actually earning 5-20% more on your property, assuming that you can keep it booked at least 80% of the time. Although you will start earning an income from the property right away, it is technically not considered profitable until the property is paid off completely. The average amount of time it takes for home owners to completely pay off their homes with Airbnb rentals is approximately 154 months or 12 years, as opposed to the average 256 months or 21.5 years when you rent out your property the traditional way. This means that most properties can be paid off in half the time with Airbnb than with traditional rentals, which is a great opportunity for people who have rental properties to get into profits faster.

CHAPTER 14

UBER/LYFT

Uber and Lyft are two different companies where people can offer to provide transportation services to other people. Essentially, if you become an Uber driver or a Lyft driver, you become a personal taxi service to customers on the Uber or Lyft platforms. Becoming an Uber driver or a Lyft driver in modern days can be a great opportunity to earn cash in your spare time as you simply offer taxi services to people who need rides. Many people earn a great profit off of this platform and because you are the one offering the services, you also get to create your own hours which means that you can easily fit this work in around what you are already doing. That being said, Uber drivers and Lyft drivers are putting in work to make their money, so this is considered linear income as opposed to passive or semi-passive income.

Why Uber and Lyft Work

Uber and Lyft work because, to put it simply, there are typically more drivers available than taxi drivers, the drivers tend to be more personable, and it is insanely easy. Instead of having to search for a taxi company's number and pay their high rates to get anywhere, people can get on the Uber app or the Lyft app and hire a driver to come directly to their location and pick them up so that they can get to their next location. Not only is it typically cheaper, but you can also take advantage of accommodations like smaller or larger vehicles depending on the number of travelers and even car seats if you have children. Plus, Uber drivers and Lyft drivers often want to put in extra effort for positive feedback so that they are more likely to get higher tips and increased bookings, so they will often do things to make your drive more enjoyable. Some of these things include offering candies, gum, inexpensive umbrellas, and even the opportunity to go through a drive thru on your way somewhere in case you wanted coffee or a meal. Of course, you will pay for your own drive thru, but the idea that they will stop for you is great.

What You Need To Get Started

Getting started as an Uber driver or a Lyft driver first requires you to apply to become a driver. Each company has their own qualifications required to become a driver, but typically you need to have a clean driver's abstract, a clean criminal record and be able to pass their basic driving test to prove that you are a safe driver. After that, you need to get the proper insurance for your vehicle so that it can be used as a work vehicle, as well as get your vehicle ready for being used as a taxi. As long as you can meet all of these qualifications, you can begin driving as an Uber driver or a Lyft driver in relatively minimal timing.

How To Get Started

If you want to get started as an Uber driver or a Lyft driver, you must first decide what platform you want to use and then look into whether or not that platform is available in your area. These two platforms are not available in every community, so it is important that you first look into this before getting into the process of getting everything else set up. Once you know that your community has either platform, you can go ahead and sign up on their website as a potential driver. You will be guided to fill out and application and shown how you can provide certain pieces of relevant documentation so that you can prove that you will not be a liability to their company. After you have completed all of this, you will need to call your insurance company and get your car insured for the proper insurance to be used as a business vehicle. You may also need to update your registration so that your vehicle is registered properly as well. Your local registry office should be able to provide you with information on how this can all be changed so that your vehicle can legally be used as a business vehicle. It is important that you do this as not having it done can put you personally at risk of major fines as well as major losses should anything go wrong. Once you have passed all of the application processes and adjusted your registration and insurance, you can go ahead and create your Uber or Lyft profile. Then, all you need to do is "respond" to potential jobs when you have extra time to make money and drive around, and start driving people to their destinations!

How Successful You Will Be

Uber drivers are said to take home $25 per hour whereas Lyft drivers are said to take home $35 per hour. That being said, Uber takes 25% of each fare for their platform fees and Lyft takes 20% of each fare. If you are choosing which one to work with, ideally you should aim to work with Lyft if you want to make more since they pay more and take less from each fare. In addition to your hourly wages, you can also earn tips from your clients, which means that you have the capacity to earn even more. How much you will earn per month depends on how much you are available to drive, so the more you drive the more you will earn. That being said, if you could contribute just 12 hours of driving per week to your Uber business you could be earning $960 per month before tips, and if you devoted the same amount to Lyft you could be earning $1,400 per month before tips. That is not a lot of extra hours to devote to earn such an incredible income from driving around!

How to Scale Your Business

Scaling your Uber or Lyft business will ultimately come from providing more hours to driving, and keeping your ratings high. The better your ratings are, the more people are going to want to book with you because the more you are doing to make their ride comfortable and enjoyable. This also means that you are more trustworthy because you have higher ratings, therefore meaning that people are going to be more likely to choose you over someone with lower ratings. Think about it: if you were about to get in the car with someone, would you want someone with a 4.5 star rating or higher or someone with a 2-4 star rating? Probably the higher rating, because this person is more likely to be a safe driver who can get you from point A to point B while also making your drive comfortable and enjoyable.

How Long It Will Take To See Profits

Exactly when you start earning profits somewhat depends on whether or not you own your car outright and how much time you are devoting to your business. Technically, if you do not own your car outright and you are still making payments on it, it will take longer for you to become profitable because you are still paying for your vehicle. However, if you own your vehicle outright, you can start seeing profits as early as that month, as long as you are driving regularly.

CHAPTER 15

SKIP THE DISHES OR UBER EATS

Skip the Dishes and Uber Eats are similar to Uber or Lyft, except that instead of driving people around you drive food around. For many people, this feels like a safer or more ideal option as they are willing to drive but feel uncomfortable having strangers in their car. If you would like to make money driving but do not want to run the risk of having potentially rude or ill people driving with you, or perhaps you are simply anxious or do not like being around other people much, this is a great alternative. While Skip the Dishes and Uber Eats will not earn you as much as Uber or Lyft would, they will still earn you a decent side income if you are willing to do enough work in your spare time.

Why Skip The Dishes and Uber Eats Works

Skip the Dishes and Uber Eats are two highly popular food delivery services that are highly favored by locals who are interested in ordering from restaurants but do not want to dine in or go pick up takeout. Thanks to these two delivery services, restaurants that never provided delivery in the past now provide delivery on many of people's favorite dishes. This means that people who previously refrained from eating at certain restaurants are now able to get food from there because they can have it delivered directly to their house. Now, rather than having to choose between Pizza or Chinese Food, people can choose between anything that is offered in their local areas, such as raw vegan food, Indian food, and even bakery foods that are now being delivered.

As a driver, driving for Skip the Dishes and Uber Eats gives you the opportunity to cash in on this lucrative deal as well, earning money for each delivery that you make. Delivery drivers are paid per delivery, as well as tips from customers, which means that they are able to earn a fair amount from each trip they make. If you want to get involved in driving action but do not want to rent out your car or have people travelling with you around the city, Skip the Dishes or Uber Eats are two great alternatives.

What You Need To Get Started

To get started with your Skip the Dishes or Uber Eats driving business, you are going to need to have a reliable car, the right insurance for your car, and an account with the company that allows you to drive on their behalf. The courier apps for both Skip the Dishes and Uber Eats are different than the customer apps, and they are used for helping you see where you need to go and what you need to pick up. You will need the courier app so that you can gain access to your account, book shifts, "clock in" and "clock out," and gain access to your delivery information. In addition to that, you will need a working cellphone that the dispatchers can contact so that they can get ahold of you and let you know where to go to pick up your next order. As long as you have these things in place, the up-front cost for getting started is actually free.

How To Get Started

To get started as a delivery driver for either Skip the Dishes or Uber Eats, you are going to need to go to the website of that company and fill out an application to become a delivery driver. The application is relatively short and does not take long to be approved. Once it has been, you will need to call your insurance agent for your vehicle and upgrade your insurance to include vehicle insurance. This is necessary because if you get in an accident with your vehicle and it is discovered that you are driving for business without the proper insurance, your insurance agent has the right to waive your insurance altogether, which can place a huge liability on you. After your application has been approved and your car insurance has been adjusted, all you have to do is download the courier app and begin applying for shifts. According to existing drivers, Uber Eats may be better if you are the type of person who last minute decides to cancel a shift because Skip the Dishes makes it more challenging for you to skip shifts without quitting your job altogether, and becoming non-rehirable. When your shifts are approved, all you have to do is wait for a dispatcher to call you and begin running the orders that you are given!

How Successful You Will Be

People who drive on a consistent part time schedule with either Skip the Dishes or Uber Eats report to regularly earn between $500 and $2000 per month from their driving. To give you an exact dollar value, most people report earning between $8-$12 per hour plus tips and after gas expenses with Skip the Dishes or $7.50 - $11 per hour plus tips and after gas expenses with Uber Eats.

Exactly how much you will earn depends on how much time you are willing to put into your driving, so that will heavily determine the amount that you earn. As well, if people choose to tip you more, you can earn more through these tips. As a general rule of thumb, driving on a Friday or a Saturday during lunch hour rush and dinner hour rush is the best time to get tips from people, and in many cases, they will tip you on the app and then also tip you cash at the door. This is a great opportunity to earn even more from your driving. Avoid working on Mondays and Tuesdays, as these tend to be the worst days for tips. If you really want to earn the most, always drive between lunch hour rushes and dinner hour rushes, as these are going to be the times when you have more people ordering, meaning that you will have more to do. The more deliveries you are driving, the more cash you earn!

How To Scale Your Business

Unless you want to put more hours into driving, there really is no way to scale your Skip the Dishes or Uber Eats businesses. These are just excellent side hustles for anyone who has extra time and enjoys driving, as it gives you an opportunity to earn some extra cash while also exploring your city. Many drivers report that they love the opportunity to see more of their city, as they are generally not exposed to the areas of the city that they discover when driving for Skip the Dishes or Uber Eats. Although this has nothing to do with profitability or earnings, it can be a nice little benefit to anyone who enjoys exploring and wants to earn some money while doing it.

How Long It Will Take To See Profits

With Skip the Dishes or Uber Eats, profits can generally be seen right from your very first trip, unless of course, you are still making payments on your car loan. In this case, technically profits are earned after your car loan is paid off. That being said, many people find that working part time for Skip the Dishes or Uber Eats is a great opportunity to earn extra income to pay for their monthly auto loan, which makes it easier for them to continue having the money to pay for said loan. This way, rather than coming out of their monthly earnings, their auto loan comes back from the car itself. This can be an intelligent way to pay your loan, or to pay it off faster if you put your entire profits toward your car loan!

CHAPTER 16

ATM

ATM machines are actually a great way to earn money. Many people purchase ATM machines and place them around their towns and earn money every single time someone does a transaction through the machine. For some people, this is a lucrative business opportunity that can help them earn more. You could even add one to another side hustle, like a laundromat, and significantly increase your earnings from that side hustle. There are many ways that an ATM can be incorporated into your side hustle to help you earn some cash without having to do anything for it.

Why ATM Works

ATM machines are a great opportunity to earn a profit because, quite simply, many people are going to need cash at one time or another and if they use your ATM machine you get paid for it. Every single time a transaction is processed through your machine you can earn anywhere from $1.50 to $5.00 per transaction, which adds up quickly if you have a machine that is well-placed. Common places for ATMs include gas stations or convenience stores, event halls, casinos, and anywhere else where an ATM may frequently be used. These are a great low-maintenance semi-passive income opportunity for anyone who wants to earn cash without having to do much to make it happen. In fact, most businesses who will benefit from having one will incorporate one into their business to ensure that they themselves are earning, even more, thus maximizing their earnings overall.

What You Need To Get Started

Getting started with an ATM business really only requires one thing: an ATM machine. Once you have your own ATM machine all you need to do is find a place to put it and then set it up. If you do not own your own place of business where you can put an ATM machine, you can always call around to local businesses to offer them to place your machine there so that you can earn an income. Typically, a business will say yes as long as they earn a percentage of your earnings to ensure that they are also being compensated for it. Typically, they will ask for anywhere from 10-40% of your earnings, which means that you would be giving them $0.25 to $1.00 per standard $2.50 transaction fee.

How To Get Started

The first thing you need to do is buy an ATM machine so that you have one that can start earning you money. You could buy a used machine, but ideally, you should buy a new one so that it is compatible with the latest technology and comes with a warranty, which means that you can earn more transactions and stay protected against malfunction or damage. The machine will likely run you anywhere from

$2,000 - $8,000. If you have more to invest, you can always buy more than one machine so that you can begin earning on multiple locations at once. In addition to owning the machine, you are also going to need to learn how it works so that you can set it up, set up the transaction fee, and learn how to keep it stocked. When it is properly functioning and delivering cash to recipients, you are going to be earning. When it is out of funds or not functioning properly, you are not going to be earning anything. Aside from that, you are going to need to make a deal with a local business to place your machine unless you have a place that you can put it yourself. If you are putting it in someone else's place of business, make sure that you keep the keys and the tools to access it, and that the business owner signs a document agreeing that it is yours. Your agreement should also outline how much you are going to give them per month to have your ATM placed so that you are both protected.

How Successful You Will Be

How many machines you have and how frequently they are being used ultimately plays into how much you are going to earn from your ATM business, but the average business will make $300 - $800+ per month per machine depending on where the location is. If you have your machine located in a favorable place that has it being used regularly, you can make closer to $800. If you have two machines located in favorable places, you can make upward of $1,600, and so forth. The things that will impact your success include how frequently it is being used, where it is located, and what the note capacity of your ATM machine is. The more money your machine can hold, and the more frequently it is stocked, the more you are going to earn in the long run, as this means that it can run several transactions before running out of cash. It is a good idea to regularly check on your machines so that you can keep them stocked, which will ensure that they are always in working order and that you can earn more from them.

How to Scale Your Business

The easiest way to scale your ATM business is to continually buy new machines and place them in areas where they are going to be used on a consistent basis. Favor businesses that have low vendor fees and high traffic so that you are earning consistent transactions and not having to give so much of your profits away to the vendors. As well, try and keep your machines centrally located so that it is easier for you to get to each machine to stock it. The more machines you can buy and maintain, the more you are going to earn through your business, so ultimately this is the best way for you to grow your ATM business. The average person with 4 ATM machines can earn anywhere from $1,200 to $3,200+ per month, making it an excellent opportunity to earn an additional income without having to do too much to keep it going.

How Long It Will Take To See Profits

The average ATM business will begin to see profits within about 12 months. Depending on how much you have spent on the machine and what you are paying per transaction to your vendor, this timespan can fluctuate. However, in order to get the best profits from your business, you are going to need to expect to keep your business going for about 12 months before you break even and begin profiting. After that, your machine will be paid back and you will start earning your $300 - $800+ per month with your ATM business.

CHAPTER 17

REAL ESTATE AGENT

Becoming a real estate agent is a linear income, however, because you are your own boss you can fit it around your existing schedule and start earning an income through real estate sales. As a real estate agent, you can decide when you are going to show homes, how many you are going to show, and what hours you are going to work. You get to set your own hours and determine your own appointments and, as such, you can easily fit this business around any other work you are already doing. Plus, real estate agents can make a significant amount of money, making this a rather lucrative side hustle if you are looking to earn a decent wage.

Why Becoming A Real Estate Agent Works

Real estate is always up, either for sale or to be bought. Regardless of whether it is a buyer's market or a seller's market, a real estate agent can earn money from their involvement in the process. Being a part time real estate agent means that you can set your own hours and do the amount of work that you want to do and nothing more. Even though you will work with a brokerage, as required by law, you are still considered self-employed which means that you are responsible for all of the work that you do. The more that you keep yourself working in your down hours, the more you are going to earn, which means that you can make a decent wage as a real estate agent.

What You Need To Get Started

Getting started as a real estate agent first requires you to become licensed as one, which requires you to go through an educational program and then pass exams and pay for your licensing fees. Your classes and exams can cost anywhere from $4,000 to $8,000 depending on where you live and what the requirements are. You also have to work with a brokerage which includes brokerage fees, which can range anywhere from 1-3% of the cost of the home you sell, as well as annual fees which can be anywhere from $1,000 to $12,000 per year. Once you have your licensing and have signed up to work with a brokerage, you need to begin finding clients to work with you so that you can list and sell homes. Most real estate agents need to do their own groundwork for finding homes to sell and finding buyers to sell to, though some brokerages will help you with advertising features built into your brokerage fee. You will need to explore what options are available to you to ensure that you are getting out in front of potential clients so that you can earn an income through your real estate agent side hustle.

How To Get Started

Getting started as a real estate agent first requires you to pass your exams. If you have not yet passed them, your first order of business is going to be looking into the legal requirements for real estate agents in your state and then meeting those requirements. Any real estate agent who attempts to get into the business without these basic legal requirements met will not be accepted by any legitimate brokerage, which means that you will not be able to get into the business of buying and selling homes. After you have passed your exams you need to find a brokerage to work through, which is a legal requirement. Brokerages are like agencies that real estate agents go through so that they can legally buy and sell land between their clients. Virtually every state requires you to work with a brokerage, so you are going to need to find one that fits your needs that you can work with before you get started. Once you have, all you have to do is begin marketing yourself in your local area as a real estate agent so that you can begin finding clients to buy and sell for. Many new real estate agents will offer referral rewards of $100 - $1,000 to anyone who sends business their way so long as those clients go through with buying or selling, as this offers an incentive for people to spread their name around. Once they grow larger in size, they often stop offering these referral rewards as they are now more well-known and can continue growing off of the existing word of mouth that they already have.

How Successful You Will Be

Real estate agents can make anywhere from $30,000 - $56,000 per year after brokerage and licensing fees if they are working 10-30 hours per week selling homes. As long as you continue advertising and working your business on a regular basis you can make an additional $30,000 - $56,000 per year on top of what you already make as a real estate agent. This number will fluctuate depending on what your brokerage fees actually are, how much you are investing in advertising, and how often you are actually buying and selling homes. The quicker you can buy and sell your home, the faster you can turn profits which means the more you will earn in the long run.

How to Scale Your Business

Scaling your real estate agent business can be done by becoming well known for what you do and having a lot of referrals sent your way. The more homes you are buying and selling for, the more you are going to earn in the long run. You can maximize your earnings by keeping your client roster full which means that you earn way more per year through your real estate business. If you find that you like selling real estate or that you prefer it to what you are already doing, you can always start selling real estate full time and begin earning $100,000 - $125,000+ per year from your business. How you decide to grow and how much you decide to grow ultimately depends on you and what you are looking for so that you can earn what is right for you.

How Long It Will Take To See Profits

Because of how costly it is to get into real estate, with exams, licensing fees, and brokerage fees, it can take about 4-6 months to break even in your business if you are working extremely part time hours (10-15 hours per week.) After that, you will be earning profits from every sale that you make through your business. You can make profits sooner, in as little as 2-3 months, if you start selling properties right away and you are putting in more hours per month. That being said, it can take some time to get the ball rolling as many people hire real estate agents by word of mouth and reviews which means that it may take some time for you to get your credibility established in your business. If you already have a decent network to reach out into, however, you can shorten the amount of time it takes you and get into sales quickly.

CHAPTER 18

FREELANCE

There are many different types of freelance work that you can get into, each of which can offer you the opportunity to start earning a side income. Freelancing work refers to any type of work that is typically done as a one-time deal with clients who are in need of an extra helping hand here and there. There are hundreds of freelance services that you can offer to help you earn extra money and, based on the nature of this work, you can set your own hours and work at your own pace. You also get to set your own wages which means that you can earn a great income through freelancing. Many people turn to freelancing as an opportunity to engage in their favorite hobbies or skills and earn some cash from it so that they can both have fun and earn an income simultaneously. This can be a great opportunity to make cash doing what you love, and potentially even lead into full time work if you set it up properly and find that you enjoy it enough.

Why Freelancing Works

Freelance works because people are always in need of additional services to be completed, regardless of what those services are. From the odd writing gig here and there to creative services like designing art or video editing, there are many different skills that can be turned into freelance work and used as an opportunity to earn an income. Many freelancers will offer multiple different skillsets to maximize their potential for working with a client so that they can receive a more significant income. The more you put your services out there and get to work, the more you are going to earn as a freelancer.

Types of Freelancing Work You Can Do

There are many different types of freelance work that you can do, depending on what you have as a skillset. The key here is to ensure that anything you offer to do for others is something that you are actually capable of doing so that people know that they can trust you and the services that you are offering. The more you can establish credibility and keep your ratings up, the more you are going to earn through freelance work, so this is important. Never list a skill that you do not have as this can lead to you getting poor reviews and losing credibility, ultimately diminishing your ability to earn an income as a freelancer over time.

To help you get an idea of what types of freelance work you can do, some common freelance gigs include things like:

- Web development and web designing
- Freelance writing and copywriting
- Creative design services (i.e. creating power points)
- Sales and marketing services (i.e. lead generation services)

- Graphic design
- Mobile app development
- Search engine optimization services (i.e. SEO and SEM)
- Branding and public relations services
- Admin support or admin assistance
- 3D modelling
- Game development
- Translation services
- Web research services
- Legal services
- Transcription services
- Writing articles or blog posts
- Customer service
- Social media coordinator
- Social media community manager (i.e. Facebook group admin)
- Logo design and logo illustration
- Audio and video production
- Data entry jobs
- Human resource management services
- Architecture services

Each of these services does require some degree of skill or background to ensure that you are capable of doing it, yet this is a rather diverse list which means that you are likely to have skills in one or more areas. Offering your services in one or more of these areas can be a great opportunity for you to offer freelance services and earn money as a result.

What You Need To Get Started

Getting started as a freelancer first requires you to have a skill that you are capable of monetizing so that you have something of value to offer to potential clients. If you already have a skill you do not need to worry about paying to educate yourself on said skill or teaching yourself how to do it, instead you can just begin offering it. Beyond having a skill, you need to market your skill to an audience of people so that you have the opportunity to monetize that skill. If you already have an audience that you can market to, such as a healthy social media audience, you can always begin by marketing to that part of your audience. Alternatively, you can use a platform like Upwork or Fiverr to get your services out to people who may be interested in working with you. Both of these platforms are like ready-made market places for freelancers to post their services and begin earning funds from people who are interested in working with you. That being said, platforms like Upwork and Fiverr do have more competitive market places and you have to pay the platform per gig that you do so that you can continue using their platform. However, if you are turning enough gigs around you can still earn an excellent profit this way.

How To Get Started

The best way to get started as a freelancer is to decide that you want to become one and then determine your marketing plan. Ideally, you should be actively marketing in one way or another so that you are getting your name out there and increasing your chances of getting discovered and earning a profit. If you are on a platform like Fiverr or Upwork, make sure that you create a solid advertisement for your services and then that you link those services to your social media accounts so that you can tap into your existing network, too. When people do begin to hire you, make sure that you do an excellent job and that you encourage them to leave a review on your profile so that people can see that you are a reliable person to hire. As you start to get jobs, make sure that you allot a reasonable amount of time each week toward completing your jobs so that you are getting them done in a timely manner and earning profits as a result. Pay close attention to detail as the better your services are the better your reviews will be, which means the more jobs you will get and the more you can charge per job in the long run.

How Successful You Will Be

Freelancers can make anywhere from an extra $500 a month to an extra $5,000+ per month, depending on how much they are charging and how much work they are doing per month. You can improve your odds of being successful by offering a wider range of services and keeping your services reasonably priced and with high ratings from people who do purchase from you. The better your ratings are and the more you are earning per job, the better your income from freelancing is going to be. If you find that you have a consistent income coming in this way and that you prefer it, you may even consider starting up your own freelancing agency so that you are acquiring clients through your own brand and you are no longer paying fees to other agencies. This way, you put the funds directly into your own pocket and you are earning a significant amount from your freelancing work.

How to Scale Your Business

Scaling your freelancing business can be done by charging more per job as you increase your credibility and become known for doing great work. The more you are known for being good at what you do, the more you can charge as your work is proven in value which makes you worth more. Aside from gradually increasing your prices, you can also do your best to keep your working hours full so that you are earning as much as you possibly can through your freelancing work. The more you are booked, and the more hours you can put toward your work, the more you are going to earn.

Another thing that some freelancers will do as they begin to book up is hiring other freelancers to work for them. If you choose to grow this way, you will be responsible for marketing to your audience and bringing on new clients and then designating certain freelancers to certain jobs. This way, you receive the money from the client and then you pay the money to the freelancer while keeping a percentage of what is paid. This can be a great way to capitalize on overflow if you have more clients than you can reasonably handle, meaning that you can scale your business and earn even more without having to do too much more work.

How Long It Will Take To See Profits

As a freelancer, you can typically see profits immediately since it rarely costs you anything to get started. If you start paying marketing fees or you pay to use a platform to market your services on, it may take you a month or two to break even, although this is rarely the case. Most freelancers start earning as much as $200 - $1,000 in their first month in business and then go on to earn upward of $1,000 per month the longer they do it. Many freelancers will even earn upward of $1,000 - $3,000 per month right from the first month, depending on how valuable their services are and how much time they have to devote to it. The more time you have, the better.

CHAPTER 19

VIRTUAL ASSISTANT

Becoming a virtual assistant means that you are working remotely for businesses, offering them services similar to that of an assistant. Virtual assistants generally cover various tasks for businesses ranging from responding to emails to setting up sales pages or creating autoresponders, and various other tasks. There are many things that virtual assistants can do for a company, although you are not required to be able to do everything to become one. As long as you have a healthy range of skills that can be of assistance to a personal brand or a business, you can earn a fairly decent profit as a virtual assistant. With more and more businesses going online and entrepreneurs rising in the online community, being a freelancer is becoming more and more lucrative, making this an excellent business opportunity for people who want to make some extra cash.

Why Being a Virtual Assistant Works

Being a virtual assistant is a great opportunity for you to earn an additional income while being able to decide on your own schedule and work around your existing obligations. If you are a virtual assistant, you have the opportunity to determine when you are going to work and how many people you are going to work for. The best part of working as a virtual assistant is that you are not generally required to work for specific hours, but instead, you are working within specific deadlines, which means that as long as you can allot enough time toward a project before the deadline is up you can go ahead and start working. This means that it does not matter if you work in the morning, in the afternoon, in the night, or even in the middle of the night, so truly you can work virtual assistant work around virtually everything.

Becoming a virtual assistant is an excellent opportunity for many people to make money from their computer as it is something that can be done at any time of the day and from any location. Since you are working remotely, as long as you have access to the internet you have the ability to make money as a freelancer. Many virtual assistants work by having just one or two live calls with their clients per month to ensure that they know what work needs to be done, followed by email support that ensures that they are staying on the same page as their clients. This means that you do not even have to worry about scheduling many specific sessions to speak with people live because most of what you do is remote and behind the scenes.

What You Need To Get Started

To get started as a virtual assistant, you really only need two things: skills, and clientele. You can become a virtual assistant by learning how to complete skills that are desirable or relevant to a specific industry or business model and then begin marketing your skills to businesses who exist in that model. A common type of person to become an assistant to is an online coach of sorts, such as life coaches or business coaches, as these are typically individuals who like to outsource their assistant work so that they can go ahead and focus on coaching clients. As a virtual assistant to a coach, to give you an example, some skills you might have included being able to respond to emails, set up automated newsletter style emails to send out to their email list, creating autoresponders on their social media accounts, scheduling social media posts, and more. These types of skills are things that allow you to do the work that a coach might not want to do but still needs to get done so that they are regularly engaging with their audience.

Once you have skills that people want, you need to start marketing to your audience. As a virtual assistant, it is typically easier for you to get into your existing network of business folks and start offering your services. Many virtual assistants will grow a network of business folk online and then start marketing their services on their platforms so that they can get discovered by the people who would be most likely to hire them. By getting in front of your audience you can easily start getting hired by people who already know you and trust you, which will allow you to earn a greater income from your business.

Skills that Virtual Assistants Have

There are two types of virtual assistants that exist: general virtual assistants (GVA's) and specialized virtual assistants who are great at a limited number of tasks. If you want to make it easier for people to hire you, being a general virtual assistant means that you can do more for a business which means that more smaller businesses will be likely to hire you. That being said, being a specialized virtual assistant means that you can charge more per gig because you are specialized with what you do and you are able to do more in a certain area of business. Some larger companies will hire special virtual assistants to do specific work because they can do higher quality of work in that area, which in turn earns the business more money. You can choose to do whichever suits what you can offer most, but make sure that whatever you offer is accurate to what you can do. The last thing you want to do is be hired by a company who expects that you can do justice to the work they need done, only to find that you are really not that good at it and they are left disappointed. Not only does that feel crummy, but it also diminishes your credibility and makes it harder for you to book gigs in the future.

To give you an idea of what skills you can offer as a virtual assistant, below are 25 different things that virtual assistants do for their clients. This list is designed to be inclusive of skills for a general virtual assistant, and even so not every single general virtual assistant needs to be offering all of these services. Still, the more that you can offer if you go this route, the more valuable you are to a company and the more work you will have to do. If you are only good at one or two things, however, consider marketing yourself as a specialized virtual assistant and charging more as this is your specialty.

The 25 skills that virtual assistants may be required to have include:

- Being able to manage emails, file them away in different email folders, and filter through the ones that are important
- Set up autoresponders or scheduled emailed newsletters on platforms like Aweber or Mailchimp
- Book appointments with clients using the company's scheduler
- Following up with clients with reminder emails for upcoming appointments and thank you letters following appointments
- Light receptionist duties, such as answering calls or taking virtual meetings on behalf of the company
- Managing the company's calendar by inputting availability and scheduling bookings or appointments into the calendar for them
- Managing the company's files by keeping documents organized on platforms like Drop Box or Google Drive
- Building databases such as email or contact lists
- Researching topics for things like blog posts, social media posts, or email newsletters

- Running personal errands, such as purchasing gifts for loved ones through online platforms like Amazon
- Booking hotels and flights for the company's upcoming trips
- Transcription work, such as transcribing voicemails, videos, audios, or podcasts
- Creating basic reports for the company, such as weekly tasks, sales, etc.
- Preparing slideshows for the company's upcoming presentations
- Liaising between yourself and other team members to ensure that everyone is on track with the work they should be doing – keeping everyone on schedule for certain deadlines
- Recruiting new team members for the company and, in some cases, training them to do their jobs
- Setting up social media accounts and keeping them optimized
- Managing and updating social media accounts on a regular basis
- Managing and setting up blogs
- Publishing blog posts that you have provided

- Filtering and replying to comments on your blog

- Answering support tickets with a platform like Zendesk

- Commenting on your blog and other blogs to increase traffic to your blog

- Participating in discussion forums or message boards on behalf of your business to drive more traffic to your business or your website

Each of these tasks is something that can support a company with growing, yet is often more than a company has time for. Especially as a brand continues to grow, having enough time to contribute to things like this can be overwhelming. Offering your services is a great opportunity to help the company keep their smaller behind-the-scenes tasks running so that they can focus on bigger things like starting and running new projects, or offering services or products that are fundamental to the business itself.

How To Get Started

Getting started as a virtual assistant is easy: create a list of everything that you offer and begin reaching out to your network to see if you can meet with anyone who is willing to hire you, or recommend you to someone who is hiring a virtual assistant. You may need to have a few samples of your services available so that people know they can hire you and get work done through you, as samples tend to show people that you offer high quality work. Designing your website or certain features on your website yourself, or offering samples of your written work is a great opportunity for you to show people how good you are at your job. You can also consider asking your early clients to provide you with reviews or testimonials after you have worked together for a while, as having these testimonies often shows people that you are good at what you do and that you are guaranteed by other clients.

If you do not yet have a network of people who you can reach out to, consider using a platform like Upwork or Fiverr to get your first few jobs from so that you can accumulate experience and reviews. After that, however, make sure that you start getting clients on your own so that you are not paying a percentage of your work fees to every single person who you work with. You can also go ahead and start joining groups on Facebook where business folks hangout and otherwise growing your network online so that you begin to have people who know you as being a virtual assistant. The more you go ahead and create these connections, the more chances you have of being hired, so continue working toward building your network. Before you know it, you will have a full roster and you will no longer have to continue working toward building your network because you will have plenty of clients to work with!

How Successful You Will Be

The biggest key to generating success as a virtual assistant is getting your name out there and letting people get to know you for the work that you do. Many people have a lot of fear around marketing themselves early on which can lead to a slow start, so be brave in coming forth as a virtual assistant and continue sharing your work with people. Talk about your business and services as often as you reasonably can and continue to let people know about the work you do so that they can continue coming to you. The more that you share with people and grow your network, the more successful you will be.

Virtual assistants can charge anywhere from $1 to $100 per hour, with the average being between $20 - $50 per hour, depending on their skill and what they are offering to a company. This means that if you work about 15 hours per week as a virtual assistant, you can make anywhere from $1,200 to $3,000 per month as a virtual assistant. The more you work, obviously, the more you are going to earn, which will help you become even more successful.

How to Scale Your Business

Many virtual assistants will scale their businesses by offering more hours per week and taking on more clients. For virtual assistants who have a full client roster and who are charging on the higher end of the scale, often their virtual assistant work earns them more than their other work does so they may choose to go full time with it. This is one great opportunity to scale your business and earn more as a virtual assistant. If you want to continue keeping this as your side hustle, however, you can either increase your wages or begin creating virtual assistant packages. Many virtual assistants will create packages that feature certain specific services either one time only or as an ongoing monthly fee. If you do this, you can offer specialized services and charge a set fee then, if you get it done sooner, you end up being able to book more clients and earn more per month. For some virtual assistants, packages are an easier way to earn more per client as opposed to hourly wages.

How Long It Will Take To See Profits

Because virtual assistant work is something that does not take much financial investment to get started, most virtual assistants begin seeing profits in their first month as soon as they hire their first client. If you have a healthy enough network, you could start seeing profits in your business as high as $1,000+ per month as early as your first month. Many virtual assistants will offer exclusive savings offers to their first two or three clients so that they can get started working and accumulating experiences and reviews, which creates an added incentive for people to hire them. If you do this and you get all spots booked, you could earn as much as $1,200+ in your first month in business, depending on what your incentives are and how long people want to work with you on an hourly basis.

CHAPTER 20

SELL YOUR PHOTOGRAPHY SKILLS

Selling photography is something that many people dream of doing, yet not everyone really knows how to get started or how to earn a profit doing this type of work. There are actually two ways that you can earn a profit from your photography skills: through selling stock photographs, or through selling photography sessions. Both ways can earn you income on top of what you already make, and are based around your own hours and what you are willing to put into the work that you are planning on doing. If you are a photographer or you are at least decent with a camera, this may be a great opportunity for you to start earning money as a photographer.

Why Selling Your Photography Skills Works

People love looking at photographs, and photography is a popular niche skill that tends to earn a fair bit of money. If you love taking photographs but do not necessarily want to book sessions and photograph strangers, you can always go ahead and start taking photographs and selling them to stock photography websites like iStock or Getty Images. These are great platforms to use if you want to earn a profit, and they work because graphic marketing is a powerful tool yet many people are terrible at taking high quality images for their businesses. Rather than doing it themselves, many people will simply purchase stock photographs from the internet and use these, which makes it easier for them to get plenty of high quality images for their website and social media accounts. If you love taking high quality images of random things or landscapes, this can be a great way to sell those images for a profit, rather than letting them eat up space on a hard drive.

If you do love taking photographs of people, or even of their animals or of their products for businesses, selling your photography skills as sessions is another great opportunity for you to earn a profit as a photographer. Many people will book clients in for customized sessions which is a great opportunity to earn a large amount of cash per session. This does tend to yield higher earnings for the photographer; however, it also does require you to be willing to have in-person sessions with people and their families, pets, or businesses.

What You Need To Get Started With Selling Stock Photographs

If you want to get started selling stock photographs, all you need is a high quality camera, a photo editing software like Photoshop, and an account with a stock photograph website or a few if you want to sell on multiple platforms. If you do not have any of the required equipment at all, getting started selling stock photography can cost you anywhere from $1,500 to $10,000, depending on what camera you buy and what quality of lenses and flashes you choose. Typically, this is a better option for people who already have a camera and who are hobby photographers who would like to earn some extra cash from their hobby.

How To Get Started Selling Stock Photographs

Once you have your necessary equipment, all you need to do to start selling stock photographs is take high quality images, edit them, and upload them to sell them on stock image websites. You will likely have to input certain keywords and metatags (a fancy name for a certain type of keyword) with your photograph so that the stock image website knows when to show your photographs to potential buyers. Then, anytime an individual or a business purchases your stock photograph you earn a percentage of the sale. Other than this, all you need to do is regularly upload new images and keep your payment information up to date so that the platform can transfer you your earnings.

What You Need to Get Started Selling Photography Sessions

If you want to earn more money as a photographer, selling photography sessions is the best way to go. With photography sessions, you can take photographs of people, boudoir, weddings, families, newborns, businesses, or even animals for people. You can offer whatever type of photography sessions you want and can act either as a jack of all trades type photographer, or one who specializes in a certain type of photography. How you choose to arrange this and what type of photography you choose to take is entirely up to you.

In order to get started as a photographer, you will need a high quality camera with proper lenses and flashes, a high quality photo editing software, a website that shows off your work and your skills, and a marketing strategy to reach potential clients. To get all of this set up you will likely need to invest $5,000+ into your business, so understand that it is a fairly expensive business to get started in. Many photographers will also offer props such as backdrops and certain costume pieces for photography sessions so that their clients can have fun themes or pretty backdrops for their sessions. If you want to do this, that will be an added expense ranging from $200 upward.

How to Get Started Selling Photography Sessions

After you have invested in everything you need to get started, selling your photography sessions only requires a strong marketing plan. Typically, the best way to get started is to take some sample photographs for people that you already know and then create an online portfolio for people to look at. This is a great way for people to get some free or inexpensive photographs while you also get some samples to show your clients how good you are at what you do. Once you have a portfolio built, you can begin sharing your skills with people and encouraging them to purchase your sessions. Some photographers will offer discounted sessions at first to increase bookings and then will offer official rates after. Once you have had your initial clients booked, you can use their reviews and, with permission, photographs from their sessions in your portfolio for future bookings. This way, you can continue getting more bookings. Generally, the best way to get out there as a photographer is through word of mouth, so make sure that you keep talking and encouraging people who have worked with you to keep talking, too!

How Successful You Will Be

How successful you will be as a photographer depends on what type of photography you choose to do with your skills. If you choose to sell stock photography, you are likely going to make around $500 per month, assuming that you have a healthy number of images uploaded into a stock platform. To earn $500 per month, you will need about 80-100 high quality images uploaded. You can earn more by having high quality images that are relevant and that are useful to people. The more trending your photographs are, the more likely they are going to be picked against the competition, so focus on uploading stuff that people actually want.

As a photographer selling photography sessions, working part time you can earn as much as $1,200 per month, as each session generally sells for upward of $125. Some people even earn more by offering professional hair and makeup services and selling packages, in which case you can earn upward of $300+ per package. This is a great opportunity for you to profit from your photography skills and earn a significant income despite only investing a few hours per month into your business. To give you an idea, the average boudoir photographer will earn $600 per package, with the package being about 3 hours long and including hair and makeup services. If you had four per month, you could be earning $2,400 per month with just 24 hours of work (this includes editing time.) If you were a wedding photographer, you could charge an average of $1,000 per session, which could be $4,000 per month if you had one wedding per week.

How to Scale Your Business

Scaling your photography business is simple: take more photographs. If you want to earn more on your stock images, take more images and upload them. Many photographers who offer professional sessions will often take images for fun or for practice and will edit them and then upload them as stock images as a way to earn an extra income. If you do this and you practice and upload regularly, you could be earning $500+ per month just from your practice photography, on top of everything else that you are doing. Over time, as your image count grows, you could be earning $1,000+ this way.

If you want to scale your business taking professional photographs, the best way is to offer great packages and increase your positive ratings. The more that you are recommended by others, the more you are going to earn as a photographer. You can also develop an online presence using social media platforms like Instagram that thrive on image sharing, as this is a great opportunity to promote your skills. Another way that people will increase their photography bookings is by offering mini sessions, where they choose a location and then go there for 8 hours and book clients for inexpensive 30 minute sessions ranging from $50 - $300 per session. If you were to book out all 16 30 minute sessions, even just at $50 a piece you would earn $800 that day. This is a great opportunity to book out otherwise slow days and continue earning more from your business.

Another way that people can scale their photography business and potentially earn money is through entering contests. Although this is not a guaranteed way to win money, many photographers enter contests and, when they win, earn some sort of cash for their winnings. Alternatively, you could print your favorite images and offer them to your clients as prints to hang in their house. There are many ways that photography can be offered as a service, so get creative and look for more opportunities to get your photography into other peoples' hands! The more you offer, the more you stand to make.

How Long It Will Take To See Profits

Because photography is such an expensive business to get into, it typically takes people 6-12 months to earn a profit from their business, longer if they are selling stock photographs as opposed to actual sessions. If you want to see your profit back as soon as possible, doing both stock images and professional sessions is the best opportunity to make your money back as soon as possible. The more you offer and the more time you have available, the better. Be sure to really leverage word of mouth and focus on building a high quality portfolio so that people are more inspired to hire you, as this is the best way to grow your business rapidly which means you get more bookings early on.

CONCLUSION

Congratulations on completing *Side Hustle!*

If you are ready to start increasing your income, getting a side hustle is a great opportunity for you to earn extra cash on top of what you are already earning every month. Earning money is a great opportunity for you to have more funds to play with, to pay off debt with, or even to invest if you are ready to start growing bigger funds for yourself or your family! Having more money is always a great thing, so choosing to invest your time in finding a way to produce a greater income for yourself is a genius opportunity to get yourself ahead in life.

I hope that by reading *Side Hustle* you were able to get a strong idea about what is available to you and how you can get started. Believe it or not, side hustles really do not have to be that challenging to get started. As well, anyone can do them! There is nothing stopping you from going ahead and getting your own side hustle started, any more than there is another person. The people who are already doing it are people who are just like you, only they have already taken the leap. You can do it too!

After reading this book, I encourage you to pick just one side hustle that you are interested in and that you can afford with your present budget and get started on it. You can invest your time into growing and perfecting that hustle until you have generated enough income and made it stable enough that you can go ahead and start another one. Continuing to stack your side hustles on top of one another, especially the passive or semi-passive ones, is a great opportunity for you to make the maximum amount possible with as little time possible, too. The more you continue developing and maturing these opportunities, the more you are going to earn without having to put in so much work! This is a great way to eventually retire your 9-to-5 lifestyle if that is what you desire and get on board with making a livable income *right now,* while also having the time freedom to actually enjoy yourself!

Lastly, if you felt that you enjoyed this book and got plenty of value from it, please consider leaving an honest review of it. Your feedback would be greatly appreciated.

Thank you, and good luck with your hustle!

Budget and Invest to

Financial

Freedom

A GUIDE TO BUDGETING, CREDIT CARD
CHURNING, RISK-FREE INVESTMENT, LOW-RISK
INVESTMENT, BEING A MINIMALIST, STOCKS,
BONDS AND REAL ESTATE

By Christopher Kent

INTRODUCTION

I want to thank you for choosing this book, *'Budget and Invest to Financial Freedom - A Guide to Budgeting, Credit Card Churning, Risk-Free Investment, Low-Risk Investment, Being a Minimalist, Stocks, Bonds and Real Estate.'* I am sure you will have a completely different perspective about your finances once you have finished reading it.

Do you want to attain financial freedom, but aren't sure where to start? If yes, then this is the perfect book for you. The reason you have chosen this book is either your finances are in terrible shape, or you foresee some financial difficulties and want to know how to prevent these or just plan for a hassle-free retired life. Either way, I am sure this book will help you.

In this book, you will learn about the basics of budgeting, steps to start budgeting, tips to attain financial freedom, setting your financial goals, understanding your financial position, steps to opt for a minimalistic lifestyle, and much more. Apart from this, you will also learn about the different types of investments according to the risks involved while investing in them. By using the information given in this book, you can see a positive change in your financial position.

So, if you are ready to learn more about all of this, then let us get started without further ado!

CHAPTER ONE

WHO IS THIS BOOK FOR?

Obtain Financial Freedom

Financial freedom is something that everyone wants, and the good news is, anyone can attain it. I mean anyone; even those who have student debt can attain financial freedom. As is obvious from the phrase, financial freedom is about having sufficient funds and a dependable cash flow that lets you live the kind of life you want. Regardless of any financial troubles that you might have today, you can always work to attain financial freedom. You don't have to worry about paying any bills or bearing any sudden expenses. Also, your debt burden is non-existent once you attain financial freedom. In this section, you will learn about the different tips that you can follow to attain financial freedom.

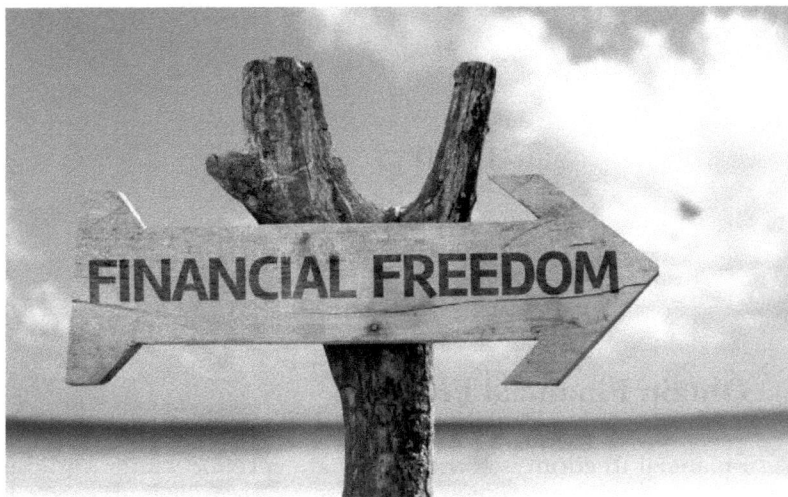

Your current position

You cannot attain financial freedom if you are not aware of your existing financial position. Working out your finances, especially acknowledging your debt, your savings, and the money you need, might not be a pleasant activity. However, this is something that needs to be done to start working in the right direction. You need to make a list of all the debts you have like mortgages, car loans, credit card bills, student loans, or any other debts. You must also include any money you owe your friends or family members. Regardless of how small the debt might be, you must make a note of it. Please be realistic while estimating your debts.

Once you make a list of all your debts, take a deep breath. This is a step in the right direction. How much is your total debt? Don't worry even if the number seems to be slightly on the higher side. The next step is to look at your savings. Include all the different forms of savings you have like savings account in the bank, stocks, any retirement fund, insurance, and such. Then, you need to add your source of monthly income like salary and any additional income you receive. Keep these numbers handy as you go through the other steps discussed in this chapter.

Phew, that's one thing out of the way.

Positive attitude

Debt can make you feel disappointed and even discouraged. However, please remind yourself that money is a good thing, even if it does seem to place a lot of burden on you at this moment. You need to ensure that you maintain a positive attitude toward money. Keep reminding yourself that with the right investment strategy and savings, you can easily attain the financial freedom you want.

A lot of people don't earn as much as they want because of the shame that is associated with making money. Money is an important part of your life, and you cannot do away with it. However, the real trouble starts when you start loving money more than anything else. Money isn't the root of all evil, but the love of money is. So, you need to ensure that you have a positive attitude toward money. You need to understand that money is like any other necessity in life, such as food or water. It helps you acquire the things you need. If you want financial freedom, then you must ensure that you start viewing money as a quintessential tool, which will help you attain your goals. If you have a negative attitude about money, your subconscious might try to sabotage your progress.

Your goals

Now that you know money is not evil, what do you need money for? Are there any specific goals you wish to attain? You might want to pay off your debts and start afresh. You might want to quit your regular job and enjoy an early retirement, or maybe you want to follow your passions. You might want to create a retirement fund or maybe save for a rainy day.

Regardless of what your reasons are, it is advised that you must make a note of all your goals. It is quite an enriching and enthralling experience to watch the progress you make toward attaining your goals. If you are trying to pay off all your debts, then it is quite motivating to watch your debts diminish while your savings increase. Every step in the right direction gives you the motivation to keep going.

However, if you don't have any goals, you will not be able to measure your progress. Also, if you want to have a sense of direction, then you need to have goals. Once you make a list of your goals and keep referring to it daily, your subconscious also starts to encourage you to work toward the end result you want. While setting goals, you must ensure that they are specific, measurable, reasonable, attainable, and time bound. If a goal doesn't meet all these criteria, then it is not a good goal. For instance, you can have a goal to pay off $24,000 of student loans within the next six months. This is a specific goal, which is attainable and time bound. If you set unattainable goals for yourself, you are merely setting yourself up for disappointment. If you are aware of what you need to achieve, achieving it certainly becomes easier.

Tracking your spending

You need to start tracking your spending if you want to attain financial freedom. You can use a different online tool like Mint to keep track of your spending and your expenses. You can also set monthly budgets for each category of expenses and see whether you can stick to the budget or not. By doing this, you will not only get a realistic picture of your monthly expenses but will also become conscious of your spending. Once you are aware of how much you spend and how you spend it, it becomes easier to cut back on expenses and spending. I suggest that you start using an app or an online tool to track your monthly expenses. Becoming conscious of your spending is the best way to start budgeting.

Paying yourself first

You might have come across the phrase "pay yourself first." If you haven't, don't worry. It essentially means that you must first save a specific sum before you can start paying for anything else. You need to pay yourself first to increase your savings. It is believed to be one of the simplest ways to create a savings for yourself. Why do you need to do this? For instance, if you set aside $1000 the instant you get your salary, then regardless of what you do with the rest, you will have $1000 as savings by the month end. If you run short of funds then you will probably need to come up with alternative sources of income to make up for other costs.

When you start to pay yourself first, you are essentially making sure that you will always have some funds to invest in yourself.

If you don't do this, your savings will never be fixed, and it is quite likely that you will only end up saving whatever you are left with at the end of the month. If you want to have substantial savings, then you must make it a point to pay yourself first. There are other ways in which you can start investing in yourself. For instance, if your employer offers a retirement savings program, then you can set up an automatic payment option where a fixed sum is deducted from your salary every month and is deposited in your retirement fund. By doing this, you can make sure that you don't neglect your responsibility of saving for the future.

Spending less

Did you know that Warren Buffet purchased a house for $31,500 in 1958 and has been staying there ever since? Given that he is one of the richest men alive today, he still lives in the same house. He can certainly afford the best the world has to offer, but, at times, frugality is important. On the other hand, Kanye West loves to flaunt his money to the extent that he once had debt worth millions of dollars. Both of these gentlemen are quite successful and rich. The only difference is that one of them didn't spend more than he needed, and it helped increase his riches.

By spending less, you can ensure that you get richer. For instance, you have $1,000 set aside for expenses. You usually spend $800 and save $200. However, if you cut back on your expenses and spend only $500, your savings will increase, and you will be able to save $500.

Experiences instead of things

This point ties back to the one listed above. Life is certainly short, and it is not about hoarding money until you are in your sixties. In your bid to save, you must not forget about living and enjoying your life. Remember that by forgetting to live, it ultimately defeats the purpose of even saving. Ultimately, the things that will ensure that you had a happy and fulfilling life are all the experiences you have along the way and not the things you own. Take a moment and think about it. The happiness you get from the things you buy is it momentary or everlasting? Does the debt created from your purchases make things easier for you? Now, it is time to rethink all this. What is your happiest memory? What were you doing and who were you with? The focus of your life must be about creating more happy memories instead of collecting materialistic things.

You might have always dreamt about traveling to Greece and might have been saving up to do this. So, go on your dream vacation and don't feel guilty about it. You didn't incur a debt to do something you wanted. Life consists of little moments like this that tend to make you happy. The best times you ever have come from spending time with your loved ones. So, it is time to rethink what happiness means to you, and it is time to concentrate on doing the thing you love.

Also, you don't have to spend the money you don't have to keep up the pretense that you do have money.

Paying off your debts

Some people might think that it is better to invest your money instead of paying off any debts. Unless you are a seasoned stock trader who always makes a profit on all your trades, it is highly unlikely that you will be able to clear your debts by making more investment. Incurring a debt will be a reason for unnecessary stress, regardless of whether you realize this or not. As soon as you clear your debts, you will certainly feel quite relieved. If you have a debt of $20,000 and have about $15,000 in the bank, you will still not be considered to be debt-free until you pay off the entire amount. Clearing your debts is certainly not a glamorous way to spend your money. However, by paying off your debts, you will be a step closer to attaining financial freedom.

The two methods of debt repayment you can opt for our snowball and avalanche. In the avalanche method, you will essentially be paying off those loans with the highest rate of interest, whereas in the snowball method, you will need to pay off the smaller debts before clearing other debts. You must decide which of these methods will work best for you. If you have multiple debts, then the snowball method might be ideal. When you can see for yourself that your debts are being cleared one after the other, it gives you the motivation to keep going. Even paying off the smallest of debts can make you feel quite good about yourself.

Paying off any debts will make you feel like a huge weight is taken off your shoulders. After you pay off the debts, you can steadily see an increase in your savings. If you clear your debts, then you can increase your savings. You can always invest even when you have debts. However, you must learn to be smart about the way you go about it.

Additional streams of income

Here is a common question that a lot of people seem to keep wondering about- "How can I ever clear my debts when I don't have sufficient income?" If you want to attain financial freedom, then you must realize that it will take time and effort. Your regular 9-5 job might not help you earn sufficient income to pay off your debts as well as monthly expenses. So, if that's the case, then it is time to consider additional sources of income to help attain your financial goals. There are two primary sources in which you can earn more - active and passive income. Active income refers to an activity like trading whereas a passive source of income is one, which keeps the income flowing with minimal effort. If you want to trade daily, then your work will be limited to only a couple of hours per day. You can become a freelance writer, a virtual assistant, pick up any jobs on Craigslist, or even become an Uber driver. You can opt for an active stream of income if you know that you will have sufficient time in the day to work on your other sources of income apart from your regular job.

If you are certain that you will not be able to devote much time, then it is time to look at passive income ideas. You can start a drop shipping business, customized items store, sell content online, rent out your property, or even become an affiliate marketer. You can use your skills to help you earn a nice additional source of income.

Investing in your future

Well, this might be the last tip in this section, but it is quite important. If you follow all the advice give up until now, then you will be debt free and might have also started to save some funds. Doing this might help increase your financial health at the moment. However, what will you do if there is an emergency to attend to? It is quite important that you create a fund for a rainy day. You must start investing in your future. You need to create a retirement fund to support your lifestyle post-retirement. You can easily make monthly contributions from your salary account toward investing in your future.

You not only must save for your retirement, but you must also start creating an emergency fund. You never know when an emergency might present itself, and you must have sufficient funds to deal with the emergencies that come your way. You will learn more about creating an emergency fund in the subsequent chapters.

How to Invest Your Savings

There are different options available you can use when thinking about investing to meet your financial goals. Each type of investment has different benefits as well as drawback and opportunities. In this section, you will learn about the different types of investment to make the most of your savings.

Stocks

Whenever you purchase any stocks in a company, you become a part owner of the company. There are different types of stocks you can invest in, and they are usually categorized according to the size of the company, type, the term of growth, and the way the stock performs during a given market cycle.

Bonds

A loan that an investor gives an organization is referred to as a bond. The company needs to pay the investor timely interest on the bond while the principal on the date of maturity of the bond remains unchanged. Different types of bonds include corporate, treasury, agency, and muni bonds.

Options

Essentially, options are contracts that offer the buyer a right to buy or sell the underlying stock, exchange-traded fund, or any other security at a specific price before the expiry date of the option. Options only offer a preferential right and aren't an obligation by any means.

Investment funds

Different funds like mutual funds, exchange-traded funds, and closed-end fund are types of investment funds. When it comes to funds, people tend to collect money from different investments and then invest those funds based on an investment strategy. Funds not only offer diversification of your investment portfolio but also allow for different types of investment strategies and styles. However, not all funds are created equally.

Bank products

Banks, along with credit unions, offer a convenient and safe way to accumulate your savings. Some banks and other financial institutions even offer services that can help manage your funds effectively. Checking or savings accounts lend flexibility and liquidity to your funds. Apart from this, a savings account also offers an annual interest on the funds placed within the savings account.

Retirement

There are various types of investments that are available if you want to save for your retirement. Not just that, you have different instruments available, which help to manage your income post retirement. For instance, a 401k is a retirement savings option which offers certain tax concessions or maybe an IRA. Managing your retirement income and saving for your retirement is an effective and necessary investment that you must make if you want financial security.

Annuities

A contract that exists between the holder of the instrument and an insurance company is referred to as an annuity. The company essentially starts to make either periodic payments or agrees to pay a specific sum at a pre-agreed time in the future. Annuities can be deferred or immediate annuities.

Alternative products

Alternative and complex products like notes which include principal protection or even high-yield bonds, tend to offer great returns. However, the risk associated with such instruments is quite high when compared to conventional forms of investment. When it comes to investing, the greater is the risk, the higher is the payout. There are different ways to invest apart from the ones that have been mentioned so far. A few of these investments have been discussed below. Investments in real estate can be made by purchasing commercial or residential property. There are REITs (real estate investment trusts) that pool together the investor's money and acquire properties. These REITs are traded just like stocks. Mutual funds and ETFs also invest in REITs. Private equity as well as hedge funds are classified as alternative investments. However, these options are available to those who meet the specifications regarding income and net worth. Private equity also allows the companies to raise the necessary capital without having to go public.

Mutual funds

This is a pooled investment and it is managed by an investment manager. It allows the investors to have their money invested in various stocks, bond, or other types of investment as has been stated in the prospectus of the mutual fund. These instruments are valued at the end of a trading day. All the transactions regarding the buying and selling of shares are to be executed after the market closes. Mutual funds can be actively or passively managed. Those that are actively managed tend to be costlier. Distributions can be made in the form of dividends, interest, and capital gains as well. These distributions of mutual funds are subject to taxation. Just like with stocks or bonds, selling a mutual fund can result in a profit or a loss. A mutual fund allows a small investor to acquire a diversified exposure to a number of investment holdings that fall within the purview of such an investment. Mutual funds allow an investor, big or small, to achieve some diversification in their investments instantly.

Commodity Futures

A commodity future is an agreement to buy or sell a fixed quantity of a commodity at an agreed price on a specific date in the future. Commodities can include metals, oils, animal products, grains, financial instruments, and currency too. Trading in commodity futures contracts usually takes place at commodity exchanges. Federal regulations allow the trade of futures contracts on single stocks and are known as single stock futures and security indices.

Insurance

There are different kinds of life insurance products available like term life, universal life, and even whole life policies. There are also variations available in each of these options.

In the subsequent chapters, you will learn in detail about the different types of investment options available to diversify your investment portfolio and increase your savings.

Measuring and Knowing Your Risk Tolerance

When it comes to calculating the return on investment, there are different variables at play. Your risk tolerance refers to your willingness and your ability to withstand any such variability. You must have a precise and realistic understanding of the risks you can and cannot tolerate. If you take on a risk that is too much for you to handle, then all it will do is end up giving you more stress. If you get in way over your head, it will defeat the purpose of investing. You must be aware of the risks you can take if you want to become a successful investor. Investing is not a gamble, especially because it involves your hard-earned money.

You can use a risk related questionnaire to assess your risk tolerance. You must consider various worst-case scenarios wherein your investments don't turn out like you hoped and the returns you get from them are disappointing. If the worst-case scenario comes true and you lose your investment, will you be able to tolerate the loss you incur? If you think you will not be able to tolerate such risks, then you need to reconsider the investments you want to make. There are several instruments to choose from when it comes to investing and you must opt for one that meets your needs without leaving you vulnerable to unnecessary risks.

There are various factors that influence your risk tolerance like your future earnings, your current financial situation, other investments you have, and the timeframe within which you want to invest. When you have stable income to depend on, your tolerance for risk will be slightly higher than those who don't have a stable source of income. As long as you have the necessary funds available, you can take bigger risks. However, the risks you take must be calculated risks and not impulsive. The risk tolerance of an investor can be usually categorized as the following.

Aggressive risk tolerance

Aggressive investors are usually well versed with the conditions prevailing in the market. They have a grasp of how securities function. The knowledge they possess is the main reason why they can invest in high-risk investments and come out as winners. High-risk investments like becoming an angel investor or investing in a venture capital funds is quite risky as the name suggests because of the volatility of such options. Investing in the securities of a company whose value can plummet to zero without any warning or expensive options, which become worthless upon maturity are volatile investments. An aggressive investor will certainly have no qualms about investing in high-risk instruments as long as the returns offered by it are sizeable. For instance, in 2014, David Einhorn of Greenlight capital valued the shares of SunEdison at $32 per share. He went ahead and invested about $480 million in that company. Due to some fraudulent accounting and other malpractices, the price of those shares plummeted to 14 cents per share in 2016. Well, that was quite a nosedive and the investor was left to bear the brunt of the crash. As mentioned, higher the risk, the higher is the payout. Well, this is possible only when things go as planned. If there are any deviations in the performance of the investment, then the risk of loss is quite significant. So, don't just jump into investing in high-risk investments if you aren't prepared to shoulder any losses.

Moderate risk tolerance

A moderate investor is someone who doesn't mind taking up risky investments, as long as they are combined with some risk-free or low-risk investments. They believe in equally spreading the risk across their investment portfolio. The most common strategy an investor with moderate risk-tolerance will opt for is one where 50% of his portfolio consists of high-risk investments and the rest is made up of low-risk or no-risk investments. This not only helps to mitigate any losses, but also helps to spread the risk across a variety of instruments.

Conservative risk tolerance

All those investors who opt for a conservative approach to investing will want to invest in assets that aren't volatile. A conservative investor will look for such investments that offer security along with liquidity. These investors usually opt for low-risk or no-risk investments. This is a good game plan, especially if you are in it for the long haul. Savings accounts, certificates of deposit, Treasury bills, and other money market instruments are the ideal options for a conservative investor. You will need to gauge your willingness to take risks.

Depending on your ability to stomach risks, you can select the instrument accordingly.

To understand your risk tolerance, you need to analyze your financial health. You will learn more about this in the subsequent chapters.

CHAPTER TWO

HOW TO START BUDGETING

About Budgeting

All of us lead a hectic lifestyle and have no time to "stand and stare" or just grab a breather, so in such situations, very few make time to plan out a budget. This, however, is very important and, if you have browsed through for any financial advice on how to make ends meet, by now you will know that there is one simple rule that pops up in every piece of advice. You need a budget. Budget, in a nutshell, is a plan to make sure your hard-earned income meets not only your day-to-day needs but also helps to prepare for unseen contingencies. Once you have a budget in place, you have pre-assigned your money for specific tasks, and that ensures you spend your money wisely. What it also does is let you see where you are leaking money due to unwanted expenses and helps you determine which expenses can either be reduced or even stopped in their tracks.

As with everything else, forming a habit is always useful, and preparing a budget helps you with your spending habits, and that is the first step toward making your money work more efficiently for you.

The very thought of creating a budget will put thoughts in your mind that it will be a complicated procedure, and whether you will be able to create one or not. Initially even with simple step by step guidelines it may seem difficult but no good was ever easy to achieve, so roll up those sleeves, and after some initial hard work, it will become a habit and then just follow the step by step guidelines provided in this book, and you will find creating a budget a very simple exercise.

So, grab a pen and paper and let's get started, the very first thing you need to ask yourself is why you need a budget? It can be any one of the following reasons or more, note down your list of reasons.

- Finding a way to save more money.
- Reduce unwanted expenses.
- Not having to argue with your spouse about money.
- Making sure your spending habits are in sync with your goals.
- Find a way to move out of the vicious paycheck-to- paycheck cycle.
- Avoiding buying things on credit (needs vs. wants)
- Getting out of existing debt.
- Creating a clear financial path for future financial goals.

Steps to Follow

I am sure I have covered some if not all of your requirements, so let's move ahead to creating a budget.

The very first thing you will need to do is list down all your expenses however big or small they may be. It does not matter if it is a daily expense or a once a year expense, you need to write it all down. Initially, it is recommended you do this exercise for one whole month and list down every expense no matter what it is. This will then give you a picture of your spending habits. There are a couple of ways you can track this. The most basic of them all is to always carry a pen and a small notepad, and every time you reach for your card or cash, make an entry. Then, at the end of the day, fill all of it on a spreadsheet. This is a more hands-on approach and also time-consuming. Initially you might even miss a few entries, so start forming a habit of keeping all your receipts to do a back check. Also, initially you can take your card statements for the last couple of months and start by adding those entries in your spreadsheet. You may not remember every transaction or what it was for, but it will still give you a broad picture of your spending habits.

There are also several APPS online, which will help you, track your expenses, and you can download the one which suits you, and that will take care of tracking your expenses. It will require a one-time effort on your part to link all your cards and accounts to the app but once done, every swipe and every withdrawal will automatically be captured for your future reference.

You may be wondering what the point of this cumbersome exercise is. How is listing all my expenses going to help me? Believe it or not, it's going to be an eye-opener for you. Let's say I ask you; do you know how much you spend monthly on food or gas? Do you think you can give me an exact figure? Chance are you won't have a vague idea, but once the budget is in place, not only will you know where your money is going but what exactly you need to do to reduce wastage and leaks from your hard-earned money.

Now that you know how to go about tracking your daily expenses, grab a calendar and mark out all the important dates for the rest of the year. When I say important, I mean all dates where you may have to spend more than your regular daily budgeted expenses, they will be:

- Birthdays
- Gifting festivals like Christmas
- Annual premiums for your insurance
- Vacations if any planned
- Taxes and professional dues
- Annual medicals
- Car repair/maintenance
- Property taxes

And anything else that you know you will be spending in the upcoming year. To help, you can check your bank and card statements for the last twelve months if you have them. If not, request a copy and that will help you identify these expenses.

One more important thing. If you have a variable income, it will be difficult to plan a budget so what you will need to do in such a scenario is to pay yourself a monthly salary. The amount can either be your average for the year of if you want to be safe the least you have made in any month. That will give you a better cushion and reduce your risk of overspending.

Identify the reason for creating a budget

Now that you have decided to make a budget, first let's find out why. It can be any one or all or more of the following reasons.

- You want to save for your retirement.
- You want to build a fund for emergencies
- You want to buy a house
- You want to buy your dream car
- You want to pay off your debt
- You want to save for college fees
- Plan a vacation

Once you have decided what your aim is, you can then customize your budget around your goals and how to achieve them. Studies have shown that setting goals helps increase your motivation and thereby increase your success rate. To be effective, you need to set absolute specific goals, like if you want to buy that dream car, it must be assigned a specific number as well like "need to save $15,000 by this date." Setting a deadline is also very important, so you know exactly how much you need to save every month toward that goal.

The more specific the targets are, the greater the chances of you succeeding, but if you have no predefined goals yet, you can decide on a random number like I will save 20% or 25% of my income and then use the same as and when required. However, based on thorough research, it has been found specific is terrific.

If you are not sure how much you need to save for retirement, college fees or how big a house you need to save for, we will be discussing this in detail in the coming chapters.

If you are single, then you are ready to start planning. However, if you are married, you need to ensure you discuss this with your partner. In some cases, there are instances where partners maintain separate finances. Even then, you will need to bring your partner on board as suddenly there may be a change in your spending habits, and your partner must be aware why. The same reason applies in case of combined finances, plus the fact that you will need to make it a team effort as you cannot stick to a plan and have your partner leaking money by spending outside of the budget.

There is no fixed order in deciding which task you need to budget first, so you can choose as per your priority all that needs to be budgeted from the detailed list below.

Retirement

Let's start with retirement and how much you need to keep aside for your retirement. So, you will need to first arrive at a figure based on your living habits, how much you will need to save to provide yourself a stress-free retirement. To put a figure to your expenses, you will need to create a sample budget factoring in your current monthly expense, plus you need to consider if your mortgage will be paid off by then or not? Will you be traveling more, or will you be content with just relaxing? Will you be taking up some hobbies that will require you to invest some funds in them? Also, something very important for you to remember will be potential health issues that can pop up after retirement. Once you have factored all of the above into the equation, you will arrive at a figure that you need after retirement. You then need to take into account any active income that you may receive at that point and deduct that from the required amount.

To calculate the income, you will have coming in post your retirement you will need to factor in three key things

- Social security
- Pension plan from the employer
- Savings
- Source of income post retirement

Social security is one of the most common and primary sources of income for retirees, but having said that, as per the last survey, the average benefit is about $1350, so you do not want to rely on this source of income alone.

Less than 20% of private sector workers had a defined pension plan a few years back. So, if you are one of the few with this option available, you need to get in touch with your plan administrator and figure out exactly how much benefit you will be eligible for. The exact amount may not be possible as the amount may vary based on your total number of years of service plus your actual age at the time of retirement, but with the help of the administrator, you must be able to arrive at a workable figure for your budget. Also, a common mistake at this stage is that people factor in their investments in 401k, etc. but that will be wrong as you are trying to calculate what amount you need to invest in producing your desired income.

Now that you have calculated two of the three key things, what you now need to do is calculate the difference between what you are going to need post-retirement and what you will be earning from the top two options, the difference that you are left with will have to come from your savings. Having said that, the aim must be the savings must be in the form of investments, which will generate enough income to bridge the gap without you having to dip into your principal amount. If you can do that, you don't need to worry about running out of cash after you retire. Since your principal balance will remain the same while you manage your expenses on the income from your investments, the returns on the investments you make will also depend on a lot of factors though some investments may give high returns initially. They may not give the same returns after a few years if they are dependent on market fluctuations, so you will need to invest in something safe, something that may give you less returns but will remain steady irrespective of market conditions. The good part about this is you will be saving a higher principal amount to do that, and that would, in turn, give you a better safety cushion after your retirement.

The above option is the simple option but what if you cannot come up with enough savings to meet the safe investments options and create a safety net? In such scenarios, you need to create a disciplined plan where you dip into your principal amount and withdraw a fixed amount every year. To do this, give yourself 30 years of retirement and calculate the principal amount accordingly. You can calculate a minimum return on this investment and deduct that amount yearly.

However, with rising taxes, healthcare costs and other uncertainties, it is always a better idea to estimate a little more than you feel you will require, the only outcome of that being that you will reach a higher savings goal and be able to lead a more comfortable life or stay afloat in case there is an emergency.

Savings

Now that you know your expenses and what it's going to take to have a life free of financial worries, let's start with saving. Unless you have money left over, you are not going to meet any of your targets so let's see how we can save some from your actual paycheck. Given below is a list of saving techniques in random order. You can choose whichever suits you the best.

Emergency fund

Emergency fund, the name says it all; it is a fund that you are going to require in an emergency. It can be a medical emergency or a sudden loss of a job, unplanned travel, car troubles or any other emergency. So, the funds need to be easily accessible as well. Typically, the amount required in an emergency fund is 3-6 months of your monthly expenses. Once you have the number, the question is where to park the funds. Investing it can result in delay if you really need the cash in an emergency and just keeping it in your bank account can easily mean a swipe of your card and the fund is gone. It has to be a combination of both. To be safe, open a separate account with no add on facilities like debit card, or even online access. Also, make sure the bank is not too close to where you live, so if you need the funds, you might have to make a short trip, but yes, the funds will be there for you. How much of the

3-6 months back up funds you want to park in your account is up to you but keep at least some part in money market funds. A Mutual fund that invests in short term securities tends to have a low rate of return but, in return, what you get is fewer fluctuations. Also, the point of having an emergency fund is not to make money, but what's the harm if they're in an opportunity to earn some interest on your saved money.

Cash envelopes

Now that you have created a budget and allocated limit for each category of your expenses, let's start with one of the basic methods, which will help you follow your plan and stick to, the limits set by you.

Please note it is very important to complete the planning stage of your budget diligently before you begin using the cash envelope system. You cannot just stuff cash in different envelopes for different expenses and expect the system to work. This step is to be used only after successful tracking of your expenses for at least a month along with backtracking of receipts wherever possible. You can, of course, tweak the amounts later but you need to arrive at a figure systematically and not just by guesswork. Once you have the figures in your budget, you will see there are two types of expenses - fixed expenses, and variable expenses.

Fixed expenses

These are expenses in your monthly budget that never change. The value of these expenses will remain the same month on month; examples of fixed expenses will include the monthly installment on your car payment, your insurance premiums, and so on. These expenses must not be a part of your cash envelope as you cannot control these expenses, and they have to be paid off monthly.

Variable expenses

All the rest of your expenses from your budget list need to be paid for using the cash envelope system. The best way to get started is to decide on the total figure you will need from your budget sheet and then on your payday go and withdraw that amount. You can add a small twist to this as well. Now that you know not just the total but the breakup of how much each envelope will require, make a list of the denominations that you will require as well to stuff those envelopes. Try and avoid smaller bills as it has been observed that while shopping people are generally reluctant to break a $50 or a $100 as compared to a $5 or $ 10. Anything that can help you save works, right!

The main reason for using cash envelopes is because it is so successful, as it is a visual system. You can see money flowing out, and your mind automatically starts to go into a saving mode. Many people do not overspend because they do not have the funds, but simply do it because they have no idea where the money is going. With a cash envelope, the moment the money starts reducing in your envelope, your spending automatically gets a bit tighter as you self-realize that you are overspending and once this money is gone, you cannot borrow from other envelopes. A classic example is when we go shopping. Most of us do not have a shopping list, and we grab what we like from the shelf and pay for it with a card. We do this without realizing what we purchase or how much we paid for it. However, with a cash envelope as you start billing and see the count steadily increasing and compare it with the money left in your envelope, the realization hits you that the money left will not be sufficient to meet your budget requirements. You will automatically put back unnecessary things like the magazine you picked up while waiting in line or the 12 pack of soda plus cookies etc. This visual aspect of watching your cash is a tremendous motivator to avoid unwanted purchases and help you buy what you need and not necessarily what you want.

Once you have stuffed your envelopes, you need to make sure that you only use each envelope for the purpose it was earmarked for. So, do not forget to either label every envelope with the category of funds or, if you want, you can get different colored envelopes to help you identify more easily what that envelope is for.

If the money in your envelope is used up and it isn't time to refill the envelope, then it can mean two things- either you didn't budget the right amount for a specific category of expenses, or you didn't stick to your budget. Either way, you must get on it immediately and find out the reason why this happened. It will take a little bit of trial and error, but in a couple of months, you must have each envelope categorized with exactly the right amount.

So, does it mean this is the end of the exercise? Well, creating money envelopes for your expenses is only one step of the process. Following this exercise doesn't mean that your finances are in order and you have financial freedom. It is merely a means of getting started and not the end of the journey. You can now do a deep dive and see where you can save. Even if you set aside a small sum, which you don't use or spend, and instead divert it to your emergency fund or let it, sit in your savings account, then you can collect it over period and use it to pay off any debts. Collect funds and use them to pay off any significant debts.

Save More

Small saving goals

Along with your budgeting and spending habits, another thing you must do is establish certain small savings goals. It can easily be achieved by making the smallest of contributions without sacrificing any of your necessary expenses. It can be something as simple as collecting all the change you get in a day and storing it in a container. It is almost like maintaining a piggybank for adults. Whenever you go grocery shopping, you must not only concentrate on what you buy, but the quantity as well. Ask yourself if you need as much as you are buying or if you can make any concessions there. If you do this, and you end up saving some money, then you must store this away for safekeeping in your piggybank.

From your existing budget, start looking for things on offer or see if certain stores are offering discounts if you make any bulk purchases. If there are any clearance sales and something you need is being offered at a throwaway price, then that's a good deal! Saving a little here and there will enable you to collect a substantial sum over time. Why don't you try practicing this for six months and see the sum you manage to save?

The amount that you collect like this is not for the emergency fund as you have already budgeted that in your expenses. Instead, this amount is to be used to get rid of any debts or reduce the outstanding bills on your credit card. Doing this over time will have a cascading effect as less outstanding will mean less interest to be paid and eventually you will be able to pay your debt off completely. This is, however, a long-term exercise, and you need to continue saving any amount that you can patiently. If you find yourself not motivated enough to save some small change, the easy way to motivate yourself is to try and make it fun. You can perhaps enter into a challenge with your spouse or a friend to see who manages to save more over a month. Ensure that the reward you set for yourself is not money related. The reward you set for such challenges can be something as simple as doing the other person's chores for a day or two. The competitive spirit will help you save more and having the added luxury of someone else washing your car or vacuuming your house is certainly an added bonus.

Short term investments

If you have now got into the habit of saving with a fixed target in mind, you can help speed things up by investing those funds. By placing the funds in short-term investments, you will not only be able to make a quick buck on the side (provided you choose your investment wisely), but it will also help you attain your savings goal. You will learn more about the different types of investments in the subsequent chapters.

Employers saving/retirement plans

In this case, you need to be aware of your company's policies. Does your employer offer employer-sponsored retirement plans like 401k, 403B, or any other plans? You must contact the concerned executive or contact the human resource department in your organization and find out all you can about this. In most cases, your employer may offer to match a certain portion of your contribution. Now, you need to find out the maximum that your employer is going to contribute and match that amount. For instance, for every two dollars you contribute to your retirement fund, your employer will add two dollars too. It is essentially a freebie that you can use to fatten up your retirement fund.

Also, your employer can deposit these amounts even before the IRS can touch them. So, this has a two-way benefit- a qualified plan from your employer not only helps add funds to your savings by matching a portion but it also helps save a lot on taxes. Only once you withdraw this money will you liable for taxes, but chances are if you are sticking to your budget plan you will not have to make any withdrawals before your retirement. So, it is a win-win situation for you. Do not pass up on this opportunity to save.

24- hour rule

You are not alone. Most Americans give in to impulse purchases, regardless of whether they are online purchases or something that caught your eye in a store. However, the more you spend impulsively and on unplanned purchases, the less you are likely to save. The solution to that problem is to enforce a 24-hour rule strictly. Well, it is quite simple. The moment you see something that will amount to an unplanned purchase, don't give into the impulse. Instead, give yourself 24-hours to see whether you still want it or not. After 24 hours, if you still feel that you need that item, then go ahead and purchase it. However, most of the time after contemplating for 24-hours you will realize that you can do without the new piece of clothing or the fancy new gadget. All this means that you will be able to stick to your budget and not burn a hole in your pocket with impulsive shopping.

Treat and save

Until now, all the options were about cutting down on your expenses and saving more. Now, let's look at a way where you don't have to stop yourself from indulging a little bit every now and then. However, there is a catch here. After you follow your budgeting strategy you might feel like you deserve to treat yourself. You might want to pamper yourself or do something, which makes you happy, and you have the funds to indulge your fancy now. Well, you can give in and indulge yourself, but there is a catch. You must save a sum equivalent to the amount that you decide to spend. Like I said, there's always a catch. This rule, when properly applied, creates a win-win situation where you don't feel like you are depriving yourself of something and at the same time, you manage to save. So, you are essentially spending and saving at the same time!

Cost in value of hours worked

The other way to put a curb on unplanned or planned

purchases which are more likely wants rather than needs is to convert the amount required into the hours you must work to earn the necessary funds. So, if you suddenly like a new pair of shoes, convert the value of those shoes into the number of hours you will need to work to pay off the cost of those shoes. For instance, if you need to work for 10 additional hours to purchase those shoes you want, it will certainly put things into perspective. The thought of extra work might change your mind about whether you want to purchase something or not. Try this method with all your non-budgeted expenses and see the new perspective you get on spending.

Credit Card

If used correctly, it is a very useful thing to have, but the very same convenience also makes it the most terrible thing to have in certain cases. We will now discuss in detail all that can go wrong with a credit card and how to handle such issues.

Once you have a credit card, you are assigned a limit for the same. Knowing that you have an available spending limit puts you at ease. You probably don't think twice before you pull your card out and swipe to make a purchase. Now, at the end of the month, if you pay it off in full then it is okay. However, if you have made a minimum required payment, that is the first step into a vicious cycle of debt accumulation. Credit card companies charge huge interest on any rollover amount that is on the card, and it continues until you pay off the entire sum due.

Most people do not even bother to look at their statements

properly and they see what the minimum due is, pay it and are content with this until the next time they feel like using the card and adding more roll-over balance on the card, thereby leading to more interest. This may feel okay to some people as it is an additional source for them to spend with other than their income, but eventually, you will reach a stage where the card limit is maxed out, and that is when the real trouble starts.

Now you do not have additional spending power but are stuck with a huge liability where depending on your card limit the huge amount of interest is being added every month without you spending a single cent on it, it puts tremendous pressure on your actual source of income to meet the minimum due required.

Once you have reached this situation, you have already dug a financial hole for yourself, and it is going to keep getting deeper unless to plan your way out of the debt. Also, at this stage, if your income does not let you make the minimum amount due required, then it is even worse. Not only will you be charged interest but there will be late fees and if the combination exceeds your card limit, over-limit fees as well. So essentially, having a credit card may seem like a good idea, but if not used wisely, you can get caught in a huge debt burden. Also to avoid collection calls, you will then be forced to resort to other types of debt to pay the minimum and keep your card current, like cash advances, balance transfers (getting an additional credit card) payday loans, etc. and what this does is dig the financial hole deeper and deeper.

Now what if you already are in this situation? Let's list down a few steps to get you out of that debt.

Firstly, you need to make a list of how many credit cards you have and what monthly amounts are due on each of them. Next you need to look at the interest rates of each card. Yes, different card companies have different interest rates. Then you need to choose the card with the highest interest rate and start making not just minimum payments but some additional amounts to help ease the burden. It's important to start getting the balance down. It can be a small amount to start with, but you have to start somewhere. Otherwise, there is no way you are going to get out of this mess unless you are willing to put in the effort to clear the debt. So, the first thing you need to do if you have any other existing credit cards with an available limit on them is to stop using them with immediate effect. Otherwise you are just going to make your problems worse. The best way to stop using the credit card if you are not disciplined enough to trust yourself is to cut them up. It may sound harsh giving up your only available line of credit, but what you need to realize is you are not just postponing the inevitable but also making the situation worse with additional debt. So rather than being in a deeper hole a couple of months down the line, you are taking away that option and disciplining your spending.

Eliminating your credit card debt

Acknowledging that you are in a financial mess is the first step toward resolving it. You have to make a workable plan and stick to it even if you do not see results immediately. Be patient, and eventually you will see the results.

Now that you have decided to get rid of your credit card debt, how do you go about it? The obvious thing is to cut down and start saving, but that alone is not necessarily going to help you. So, you must first see how bad your situation is and whether you can manage it by cutting down on a few luxuries. If being a little frugal works, then that's great. If it doesn't, then sit down with a pen and paper and list down all the cards that you have and the current outstanding balance on each of them. See which one has the highest interest. Though it may sound like just juggling your outstanding balances from one card to another, see if there is a card with any limit available and which gives you an option of balance transfer. The reason for a balance transfer is that companies want you to have your outstanding debt with them so they can charge interest and make money. To do that, they give you attractive offers like transfer of your balance from another card onto this particular card. They will probably charge zero interest for a period of 60 days and, in some cases, even longer periods. If you use this option wisely and with discipline, it can be your first step toward reducing credit card debt.

Let's say you do have this option available to you. You need to transfer the outstanding balance of the card with the highest interest to another card, preferably with lower interest. However, at this point, it does not matter because of the limited choices available to you. Once done, this card is essentially paid off and for the other card, you will need to continue the minimum payment you were already paying before the balance transfer. If you do this, nothing changes and after the free period, you are back to repaying your debts. However, what you need to do is utilize the interest-free period with a vengeance and try to save as much as possible and put it all on this card. You will not be able to pay off the

156

complete balance but what you will manage to do is knock off a big chunk of the sum payable with significant interest piled on top. You can repeat this exercise until you pay off your outstanding amount. However, if the amount is just too big and you see that this option is not going to solve your problem, then you need to look at alternatives. You may even find that you can do this transfer at a time when you have overtime or extra income. That works in your favor because when you pay off more than is due on the new credit card balance, at zero percent, you effectively drop the amount that you owe to a manageable level.

Before we look at the alternatives, there is another approach to this, and that is to take the card with the lowest outstanding amount and aim toward getting rid of that balance first. You must do this regardless of which card is charging the most interest. The reason for this is, although you may end up paying more money on interest trying to clear the outstanding balance on a card, it will give you the confidence to keep going. Apart from this, it will also help improve your credit rating, which in turn will open up options for you to resolve your debt issues. This is called the "snowball" effect and as you clear one small debt, you move onto the next smallest debt, so as to eliminate these.

Perhaps you have gone through your card statements and concluded that balance transfer is not going to be an option. You do not have any limit to play around with, and your credit is so low that you cannot apply for a new card to work with a balance transfer option. In such a case, you will need to seek some professional help and work with a credit-counseling agency, preferably one that is a non-profit organization. You can also borrow money from your retirement account like a 401k, borrow against your car or house, or explain the situation to a family member explaining the seriousness of your intentions to resolve your credit issues and take a loan from them.

Debt Consolidation

You need to try debt consolidation when you have tried every other method to try and resolve your debts but are unable to do so. With your credit cards maxed out, chances are your credit score will also have been affected. Getting further credit in the form of new credit cards or loans will not be that easy. In such cases, you must try and pick the best lenders who offer the best rates for debt consolidation. This way, you can relieve yourself of the stress and worry of making multiple payments and will only have to worry about making one set payment. It will also help you potentially save hundreds if not thousands of dollars in interest.

Debt consolidation agencies offer different services and some of them have attractive offers like less interest chargeable or no prepayment fees. However, all this depends on how good your current credit score is. So, after researching, choose the one that suits your profile the best. If it looks like your situation is beyond repair where you have not only maxed out your cards but have missed payments too and your credit score has almost hit rock bottom, you may then want to consider Debt consolidation through a DCA or Debt Consolidation Agency. Be sure that the payments that are expected each month suit your income so that you can meet them easily.

Debt Consolidation Agency

Now that it is well established that you alone cannot handle your debts, it is time to take a little professional help. Just because you have maxed out your credit cards and your credit score are low does not mean there are no alternatives. There are still a few options you can try. There are specific debt consolidation agencies that, in spite of a low credit score, are willing to give you a loan to pay off all your debts, and then you have to make a single payment to them every month. Though this option might turn out to be slightly costly initially, it is all that you are left with. Right now, you are left with very few other choices, so go ahead and take what you can and work out a plan that allows you to have a little left over after paying the loan and after accounting for your budgeted costs. This may be a slow, painful process, but it starts to get you working in the right direction. This should make life easier, because you no longer have creditors hounding you. The other advantage is that you only have to make one single payment which is easy to track and if you have created a program with your DCA that suits your current financial situation, you can start chipping away at this loan by adding that additional cost as a part of your budget.

Now let's say you don't qualify for a loan from a DCA either. This means that you are in a bad spot and that's before you even begin budgeting your expenses. You need to find a way to get from one day to another, in a situation this grim. Below are some options, which may work if you have not thought of them already.

DSA- Debt Settlement Agency

The main reason you must choose a DSA is that once you have registered with one, they handle all the negotiations of your debt on your behalf with the creditors in an effort to try and settle the debt at less than the due amount. No collection agency can call you in regard to debt once you are registered with a DSA. That in itself will ease a tremendous pressure leaving you free to try and earn more. The way this works is the DSA will now call up your creditors on your behalf to try and settle your accounts for a value less than the current amount outstanding. What you need to note is this is applicable only if you have been defaulting on your loans and have not made payments for a few months on your cards. This option will further harm your credit, but right now, this will be a good way of getting out of debt and then learning from your past financial mistakes to make a fresh start with your budget.

Refinance Your House

This is an option which is the most convenient but also the one which most people don't realize that they have. Yes, you have a mortgage on your house, and yes it has not yet been paid off, but what people don't realize is that property prices tend to appreciate over time and you may be eligible to get a refinance loan for the difference between the amount outstanding on the house and the value of the house. Also, with refinance the amount can be high and interest low, allowing you to either pay off all your debts and start afresh on your budget or at least pay some and settle some depending on your situation. Either way, your situation improves. It is important to realize that if you do not make payments on time for the remortgage, you could lose your home, so make sure that you do not take on more than you can easily afford to pay.

Loan against Your Vehicle

If you do not have a mortgage or enough equity to refinance, you can see if there is an option to take a loan against your vehicle. There are many banks and credit unions you can approach to do this. Any additional money will help you get back on track for some time at least and give you a chance to change your financial situation and start adhering to your budget.

Save on your Utility Costs

Another form of saving that many generally tend to overlook is saving on utility bills, and it does not even take that much of an effort to do this. Now that you have created a budget, you are already aware of exactly how much you have been spending on utilities. Try the following steps, and any money that gets saved gets apportioned to the most required section of your budget, whether it is your retirement fund or your emergency fund, etc. you will have prioritized the requirements by now.

- Reduce the temperature
- Try a ceiling fan
- Use windscreens to eliminate dust

- Replace your filters
- Try alternate methods of cooking
- Buy energy efficient appliances
- Make your home leak proof
- See if you can use solar.
- Reduce the temperature

It does not take a rocket scientist to figure this one out, yet most choose to ignore this obvious solution. Once the thermostat is set, no one thinks about changing it. However, if you reduce the temperature when you are stepping out of your house or when you are nice and cozy under your blankets, you can start saving. It has been estimated that for every eight hours of reduced temperature, as low as one degree, this can help lower your electricity bill by one percent.

If you are in a climate that does not require heating but just the opposite, don't immediately reach for the air conditioner. You can install some ceiling fans. Though installing the fans does not reduce the actual temperature, it does provide relief from the heat by circulating the air in your room. If this does not help, you can try a combination of AC and ceiling fan to help you out. Any small saving will eventually add up.

You can start using windscreens. The main reason for this is not to keep your windows open to let the air in and cool your house, but dust hampers the function of your appliances as well. When you are stocking your refrigerator, once in a while check to see if the coils below are blanketed in dust. These need to be cleaned regularly as a dust-covered coil needs to put in that much more effort, thereby leading to that much more electrical consumption.

Similarly, you must check the filters on your AC unit regularly. These trap the fine dust particles from the air before going onto the blower, giving you clean, cool air. However, as the dust becomes too much, it becomes an effort for the AC to pull in the air as the access is completely blocked by dirt, this puts additional load on your AC. The result, as you must have guessed by now, leads to higher electrical consumption.

By following these simple steps, you can significantly reduce your utility bills.

CHAPTER THREE

BECOMING A MINIMALIST

Benefits of Minimalism

Minimalism is all about reducing clutter in your life so that you can start focusing on things that do matter. It is not just about eliminating physical objects, but is about decluttering your life mentally, physically, emotionally and even financially. Once you embrace this lifestyle, you can shift all your focus toward things that do matter. When you do this, you will be able to see all the opportunities that come your way. By opting for a minimalistic lifestyle, you don't have to stop spending money. Instead, you will learn to spend money only on the things that you need in life. All this will help maximize the benefits. In this section, you will learn about the different benefits minimalism offers.

Prioritizing your spending

Minimalism allows and encourages you to embrace all the essential things. This habit will naturally translate into the way you spend and how much you spend. If you are not keen on acquiring materialistic possessions, then you will start to concentrate on experiences. This will change the way you

164

spend your money. By understanding what matters the most to you, you can change your spending priorities, and only concentrate on what you need. All this helps increase your savings while making you more conscious of your spending habits.

Reduces your need for things

When you embrace a minimalist lifestyle, you start to limit your need for things. Since you buy fewer items or own less, it is an effective means to decrease your spending and increase your savings. It can also mean that it becomes easier to clear your debts and attain the financial freedom you desire. If your purchases decrease, you can easily divert those funds to your savings and investment. It helps you focus on attaining your financial goals without making you feel like you are depriving yourself of anything.

You will need less

By embracing minimalism, your need for storage space decreases. As you start prioritizing your belongings and only hold onto the things you need instead of all the clutter you have gathered over the years, you will need less room. When you declutter, you will realize you don't need a lot of physical space to live in. This, in turn, helps to cut back on the mortgage or rent you pay for a huge house. I don't mean that you need to shift to a smaller house, but that you always have an option of shifting to a smaller house. It is not only cost effective but will enable you to concentrate on things that matter.

Helps focus

Minimalism and mindfulness go hand in hand. Mindfulness is an added benefit of minimalism. It is a quality that comes in handy while budgeting and creating your financial goals. Budgeting is all about spending according to a plan based on your current priorities. Once you understand what matters the most to you, it becomes easier to decide how much and when you spend your funds. It also helps you notice all those areas in life where you need to change your spending habits. By changing your spending habits and increasing your savings, you can easily attain financial freedom.

Clear your debts

A simple way to get your finances in order is to clear all your debts. A lot of people start to clear off their consumer debts when they adopt a minimalistic lifestyle. As you get rid of debts, it stabilizes your finances and gives you some flexibility. Also, by reducing your debts, you can breathe a sigh of relief. You can use all the funds you are left with to do something you are passionate about. For instance, if you don't have any credit card bills to pay, you can use those funds to increase your savings or investments. Also, when you are aware of all your expenses, you can make provisions for these and cut back on your credit card use.

Sell what you don't need

If you are just getting started with minimalism, then the best way to declutter is by selling everything that you don't need. You can use the funds from the sales proceeds to free up any clutter in your financial life. Maybe you can use the funds to pay off any small debts, start an emergency fund, or even use it for going on a trip you have always wanted to! As you start decluttering your life, you get a chance to fix any financial mistakes you made in the past. Organizing a garage sale is a rather simple way to get rid of all the clutter and make a quick buck on the side.

Simplification of your finances

There are different things you can do to get a handle on your finances. You can start paying your bills on a single day or start using cash for your daily purchases. By doing this, it becomes easier to keep track of your expenses as well as how much you spend. You can also start using different online apps or expense tracking tools to help with the budgeting process. It helps ensure that you are sticking to your goals and aren't overspending.

Giving becomes easier

When you are aware of all that which matters to you and have a hold on your finances, it becomes rather easy to give. Giving can be in terms of time or even monetary help. When you embrace minimalism, it becomes quite easy to see what and how much you can give without putting yourself in a tight spot. A simple change in your mindset and attitude toward finances can help attain your financial goals.

Become a Financial Minimalist

A lot of people actually feel that their finances control them instead of it being the other way around. After going through the previous section, I am sure you must be excited about embracing a minimalistic lifestyle. In this section, you will learn about various practical tips you can use to become a financial minimalist.

Consolidating your bank accounts

You can get by fine by just maintaining one savings account and a checking account. If you happen to have more accounts, then it is a good idea to consolidate all your accounts into one savings and one checking account. It helps simplify all the banking process you undertake without losing out on anything. This stands true for your retirement accounts too. If you have multiple accounts because of any previous employment you held with various 401k plans, then you merely need to consolidate them all into one self-directed IRA account. This reduces all the paperwork you need to do and also makes it easier to get an accurate picture of your total savings.

Reduce your paperwork

As mentioned earlier, if you have multiple accounts for different financial investments, it means your paperwork will start to pile up. It can get to a stage where you no longer have the time to go through it all. Not just that, having a lot of paperwork to tackle merely increases your stress. By getting rid of all unnecessary paperwork and keeping only that which is a necessity, this will save you time and effort. In this modern world, you can check most of your transactions and statements online. If you are consolidating your accounts, then your paperwork will naturally reduce. Try to opt for all online banking services instead of the manual offline ones.

Number of credit cards

A lot of people tend to have multiple credit cards. These shiny plastic cards are like a Pandora's Box. If you lose track of your finances, you can get in way over your head and might not even realize how far in debt you are. Having a lot of credit card debt can effectively ruin your credit score too. By maintaining only one credit card, you will become aware of your expenses and your dues too. Not just that, it is a great way to declutter your financial life. You must opt for a credit card that offers the best benefits and let go of all the rest.

No debts

Debt not only costs you money, but it does make your life quite complicated. If your debts are too high, then your finances will start to control your life. This is certainly not a good way to live. Not only will you be spending all your time trying to pay your bills, but it also increases your debt. It is quite easy to lose control over your debts if you aren't careful. Apart from this, if most of your income goes toward the repayment of the debt, you will not be left with much, and it can make you feel overwhelmed. So, by eliminating your debts, you can make your life a little less complicated. One of the best ways to adopt a minimalistic life when it comes to finances is by becoming debt free. This isn't an overnight process and will take some time. However, if you focus on your goals and stick to your plan of action, you can be debt free.

Investing

It is certainly more exciting and rewarding to invest in individual stocks instead of funds. However, it can get quite messy. You must do the necessary research, buy the stock, actively track its progress, and then sell it at the right time. You must do these things for every stock you own. If you own a couple of dozens of stocks, it can quickly become a fulltime job, even if you aren't interested in it. You can do away with all this hassle by selecting to invest in mutual funds. Funds are not only easier to manage, but it is quite easy to stay on top of all the tax requirements.

Reduce your expenses

The best way to adopt a minimalistic attitude toward your finances is by reducing your expenses. To do this, you must first become aware of all your expenses. Go through the information given in the previous chapters to make a list of your expenses. A simple way to reduce your expenses is only to purchase those things that you need rather than things you want. If there is something that you feel like buying right now, wait for a month and see how you feel about it then. If you still feel like buying it, then you can. However, most of us tend to be impulsive shoppers, and by keeping your impulses in check, you can easily break free of consumerism.

Instead of eating out every day, you can start eating at home. Cooking your meals at home is a great way to reduce your expenses. Not just that, it also helps ensure that you eat healthy meals. If you are used to spending $5 every morning on a cup of coffee, you can start brewing coffee at home. If you spend $5 per day, that amounts to about $1800 per year! That's a lot of money you can save if you make coffee at home instead. You can start using public transport and walk short distances whenever feasible. You can also start eating common meals. A simple tip is to establish a weekly grocery and expenses budget for yourself and stick to it.

Paying cash

It might sound rather old fashioned, given that going cashless seems to be the latest trend. Well, paying for your expenses with cash is a great way to become mindful of your expenses. When you pay with cash, then it becomes easier to keep track of your funds and expenses. When you go cashless, it is quite easy to lose track of your spending until your bills arrive. Whenever you make purchases using cash, you merely need to make your purchase and that's that. You don't have to worry about dealing with any payments to be made later or going through any bank statements. Also, it becomes easier to allocate a budget for your spending and stick to it. Only use your credit card when it becomes crucial and for any significant transactions.

No unnecessary services

Most of us tend to have a lot of subscriptions we pay for monthly for services seldom used. If you are paying for a gym membership that you never use, then it is time to either end that subscription or start using it. If you have subscribed to multiple online streaming services like Netflix, then hold onto the one you like the most, and do away with the rest. By eliminating such unnecessary expenses, you can start saving a little. Also, fewer subscriptions mean you must make less payments, and this is an easy way to manage your finances.

Restrict your goals

It is quite essential to establish specific goals and work toward achieving them. However, you cannot be successful if you set more goals than are practically attainable. It is critical that you set one - or at the most two - critical goals. Anything more than this and you will lose track of what needs to be done. Your concentration is like a bucket full of water. Every distraction is like a small hole in this bucket. If there are too many things you need to concentrate on, then there will not be any water left in the bucket. Setting too many goals is an easy way to lose focus on what is essential in life. Multiple goals tend to spread out your fixed assets like time, resources, and energy. Not just that, but it will also cause unnecessary confusion. To avoid all this, you must set a goal, attain it, and then move onto the next goal.

Increase your income-generating activities

This tip usually applies to all those who are self-employed like freelancers. If you hold a 9-5 job, then you will have a fixed source of income. However, if you want to increase your productivity, then you must start concentrating on all those tasks that directly contribute to your monthly income. When you make a list of such tasks and jobs, it becomes easier to do away with the unnecessary tasks that don't contribute to your bottom line in any manner.

Too much information

Information is essential to make informed decisions. However, too much information can be a bad thing since it causes a lot of needless confusion. Too much noise only increases mental clutter. You need to know when to stop. Everyone will have different opinions and different self-proclaimed "financial gurus" will give you various advice, which might not be suitable in your given situation. So, if you find something that works for you and you have a good feeling about it, stick to it. Don't overwhelm yourself with unnecessary information.

CHAPTER FOUR

WHEN MUST I INVEST?

Should I invest if I Have Student Loan?

Well, it is a common belief that it is a good idea to pay off your debts before you think about investing. This becomes rather tricky, especially when you have significant debts like a student loan. You might think that you must first pay off your student loans once you start working and only then invest. However, is this the best way to go about doing things? Do you need to wait until you are debt free before investing? Or can you invest even when you have student loans? You will learn the answers to all these questions in this section.

When it comes to personal finance, there isn't one solution that can fit everyone's needs. You must analyze your current situation and then decide the best course of action. You must consider important factors like tax deductions, expected rates of return on investment, and the risks involved. Here are a couple of factors you must keep in mind while you debate about whether you must repay your student loans or invest.

Compound interest

Interest doesn't have to be a bad thing necessarily. Most of us think it is terrible because interest starts kicking in on the student loan payments as soon as you start working. For instance, when you graduate with student debt or when you start using your credit card, a portion of the payments made is for the interest due on it every month. This can hinder your ability to repay your debt quickly and can end up increasing the duration of the loan. However, interest can be your ally when you earn it.

This is precisely what investing is about. You will essentially be making your money work for you and derive the benefits it offers. After a while, the interest on your investments tends to add up, and you will be pleasantly surprised with the sum you have earned. To do this, you must first consider if you can get a better return through investing than what you will save by paying off your student debt.

Depending on when the loan was taken along with the type of loan, the interest rates can be between 4 to 8%. Repaying your debt is as good as seeing a guaranteed return. For instance, the sooner you pay off a 5% student debt, then sooner you can start saving. However, what if an investment offers you a 7 to 8% interest? When you make a long-term investment with a reasonable rate of interest, then it will make it worthwhile to invest while paying off your student loans.

Tax deductions

Another point you must consider are the tax benefits you can claim if you invest while repaying your student loans. According to your eligibility, you will be qualified to make a deduction of up to $2500 on your taxable income. Over time, this will make the interest payable on your loans less expensive.

175

When it comes to numbers, the option of repaying your student loans or investing can be easily made by comparing your interest rate after taxes.

You can estimate your interest rate after taxes by using this simple formula:

Student loan interest rate X (1-marginal tax rate).

If the interest payable on your student loan is 5% while filing income tax as a single individual, and your income is $50,000 a year, then it places you in the 22% bracket for 2019. By using the formula mentioned above, you will get an interest rate of 3.9%. So, essentially, the interest rate payable on your student loans is about 3.9%.

So, if you manage to get an annual return of about 7% on your investments, then you can easily make up for the 3.9% interest payable toward the student loan. If the numbers work out favorably, then it is a good idea to invest while only making the minimum repayments on your student debt.

List your priorities

Not everything is related to numbers, and you must also consider your priorities while thinking about repaying your student loans or investing. Some essential goals you might need to include the following.

You might need to consider saving up for any emergencies. It is quintessential that you create an emergency fund. You need to save up at least a couple of thousand dollars as an emergency fund before you think about working toward any other goals. If you have any high-interest debts, then it is a good idea to clear those dues before anything else. For instance, if you have a credit card debt at 17.99% interest, then repaying it is a wise choice. Apart from this, you must also consider how much you want to start saving for your retirement. Creating a nest egg is essential to secure your future. You might also have some significant life plans like getting married, buying a house, or even starting a family. Make a list of all your priorities along with the funds they require. Once you do this, you can get a read on your financial situation. You can then consider whether you need to repay your student debt before investing or not.

Is 401k Sufficient for Retirement?

A 401k plan enables employees to make certain deductions from their salary as a contribution toward their retirement fund. Most of the 401k plan deductions are made before taxation, but this differs from one employee to another. Your employer can either match your contribution to the 401k plan or even offer to make a non-elective contribution. The earnings or contribution toward the 401k are on a tax-deferred basis.

Usually, there are specific caps placed on the contributions, which can be made to the 401k. The Internal Revenue Service or IRS has specific regulations in place that limit the percentage of salary that can be a 401k contribution. In 2019, the cap on 401k contribution is set at $19,000, and it is $500 more than the previous year's limit. For an individual making $150,000 per year, the 401k contribution gives them a savings rate of about 12.7%. If your income exceeds $150,000, then the savings rate tends to reduce. Having a savings rate of about 12% is certainly not ideal to meet your requirements post-retirement.

The cap on contributions to a 401k for the year 2019 is $56,000 from any source, and for those over the age of 50 years, they can add the contribution of about $6000 as a catch-up contribution. All contributions to the 401k need to be made before 31st December.

So, a 401k plan might not be sufficient for your retirement, and here are the reasons.

Taxes and inflation

The cost of living is never constant, and it has been increasing steadily. A common mistake made while calculating the retirement requirement is that a lot of people overlook the effect of inflation. Retirees tend to think that they have plenty of funds in their retirement funds or 401ks. They think that they have financial freedom and then the hard reality hits them. The cost of living increases while their funds stay the same. Even if it might sound like you have sufficient funds at the moment, this requirement will change because of inflation.

Apart from this, there is the problem of taxes that you must not overlook. An advantage offered by 401k is that it is tax deferred. It essentially means that the 401k will grow without accrual of taxes. However, once a retiree starts to make withdrawals from the 401k, the same will be added to their yearly income, and it will attract income tax at the current rates at that time. This rate, just like inflation, will probably be higher than what was assumed by the retiree 20 years ago. The 401k created by an individual during their 20s or 30s might not turn out to be as bountiful as they might have hoped.

All the money in the 401k is tax deferred. It means that for every dollar you save now, it will only amount to be about 65 to 80 cents depending on your tax bracket. So, if you save a million dollars, it will not necessarily mean that you have a million dollars to spend after retirement. You need to save in the 401k with a margin of at least 30% if you want to maintain the lifestyle as you do now.

Other fees and costs

The fees and other costs associated with the 401k can be quite steep at times. These costs can affect your bottom line and even reduce your savings. There are several fees that are left undisclosed, like bookkeeping fees, legal fees, finder's fees, and trustee fees. This can easily overwhelm you, and if you aren't careful, you can get fleeced. This is apart from any other fund fees payable. Mutual funds included in 401k tend to charge an outright fee of 2%. If a fund gives you a 7% interest but then charges you a fee of 2%, you aren't left with the kind of returns you will have expected. So, if you aren't careful, it can run into thousands of dollars that you will lose out on. If you want to save, then you need to take into account all the charges payable while calculating the savings you are making.

Lack of liquidity

Mostly all the funds that you put in the 401k account are safely locked away, and they cannot be fully accessed until the individual reaches a certain age or when they have an excellent reason to incur the penalties on an early withdrawal. Unlike other forms of investment, a 401k account doesn't offer any liquidity. You must not think of your 401k as an emergency fund or an account you can dip into to finance a major purchase. If you ever need to make an early withdrawal from this account, the charges you incur are rather expensive. If you make a withdrawal before you are fifty-nine and a half years, then you will be attracting a 10% penalty. All the withdrawals are taxable, and the amount of tax payable will depend on the income bracket you fall under. The higher the tax bracket; the higher the taxes will be that you need to pay. It is not possible to invest or even spend money for cushioning your life without incurring a significant financial expenditure. However, borrowing from the 401k is an exception to this rule. You can certainly borrow money from your 401k, but it is a short-term loan. Also, you need to repay it within a fixed period and the period given in usually sixty days.

So, what's the bottom line? A 401k will certainly help accumulate funds for your retirement, but it might not be sufficient. As prudence suggests, it is a good idea to make other investments to make sure that you have a comfortable investment. You must never place all your eggs in one basket, and by having a diversified portfolio of investments, you can ensure that you have the financial freedom you desire even in your retirement.

Setting up an Emergency Fund

Building an emergency fund not only takes time, but it requires dedication too. An essential part of becoming debt free is setting up an emergency fund. A lot of people have different opinions about how to go about doing this. For instance, it is a general belief that your emergency fund must have three to six months of your earnings as savings. As long as you only think of it as a general rule of thumb, it is fine. However, it can take people a couple of years to attain this goal. Also, while saving for this, how can they manage all their other expenses? Is it sufficient to only save three to six months' worth of income?

How much must you save for emergencies?

According to the famous finance guru, Dave Ramsey, it is better to start with $1000 and then tackle your debt. If your monthly expenses amount to $10,000, then by saving $1000, you can only cover an emergency that spans over three days. Well, this doesn't sound reassuring. Instead of searching for a magic number, you must consider different factors while deciding the amount you need to save for a rainy day. In this section, you will learn about the different factors you must consider, and they are as follows.

A financial catastrophe is something you cannot afford to ignore while setting up an emergency fund. If you have a mortgage on your apartment and then lose your job due to unforeseeable conditions, then it might mean moving back with your parents. Always prepare for the worst-case scenario while setting up an emergency fund.

You must consider the interest rates payable on any debts you have. For instance, if you have a significant credit card debt carrying an interest of over 18%, then the best thing you can do is start clearing up your dues as quickly as you possibly can. If the interest rate on your debt is comparatively low, then you can pace your repayments accordingly.

The amount that you need to set aside for an emergency fund will also depend on your access to cash if an emergency presents. If you cannot easily access a line of credit or get your hands on the funds you need in an emergency, then the amount you set aside for a rainy day needs to be rather substantial.

Nothing is guaranteed in life, and there will be circumstances that can easily catch you unawares. The risk of losing your job is a real possibility unless you have permanent employment. That is quite rare, and the risk of job loss is a possibility that you cannot afford to ignore. There is no fundamental rule that you can follow, and you need to analyze your situation while making any plans carefully. If you have good enough job security, then the amount that you set aside for an emergency fund doesn't have to be too large.

If you have several sources of income, then you can consider the option of paying off your debt while maintaining small savings. Your job stability, along with your source of income, can influence your emergency fund requirements. Apart from this, another thing you must consider is the 401k plan. Does your employer make matching contributions to it? Then this is an excellent way to start creating a fund for your retirement. However, as mentioned in the previous chapter, this must not be the sole source of retirement funds.

Steps to build an emergency fund

Here are the different steps that you must follow while creating an emergency fund for yourself.

Track your income and expenditure

The first thing you must do is start by saving an amount equivalent to the expenses you incur in a month. This amount must include any sum that goes toward investing or debt repayment. Once you save funds equivalent to one month's expenses, you need to split any extra money you are left with between repaying any debts and adding it to your emergency fund. If your employer matches your contribution to the 401k, then you must try to make the most of it and build it up on that. By doing this, you will be able to effectively save, invest, and even pay off any debts you have.

You need to start tracking all the expenses you incur in a month along with the income you earn. You can use an online tool or an app like Track Your Spending to do this. If you want, you can also make a note of the same in a journal. By making a note of your expenses and income, you will get an idea of how much you spend and the amount you can save. You must include all recurring expenses like insurance premiums, mortgage payment, utility bills, and even make provisions for expenses like childcare and any other expenses you can incur when you go out.

Setting a goal

Your emergency fund must cover at least three to six months' worth of your expenses, i.e. the amount you set as a goal for your emergency fund. If you feel that you have a stable source of income or have access to any quick means of funds, then your emergency fund can be a slightly lower figure. You must set a goal. If not, the chances of procrastination setting in are quite high. Set a realistically attainable goal for your emergency account.

Plan of action

Once you set a goal, you must develop a plan of action to attain that goal. You can include certain measurable and specific goals to work toward. For instance, you can set a goal of increasing your monthly contribution to the emergency fund by about $150 per month.

Accessible

The emergency fund that you create needs to be easily accessible too. If you place your funds in a place where you cannot access them, it will become rather difficult in case of an emergency. For instance, if you save your funds in the form of a real estate investment, then the liquidity it offers isn't high. However, if you save your funds in the form of cash, you can readily access it as and when the need arises. Saving your funds in a savings account in a bank is a good idea. You will not only be earning interest on your funds, but it is a risk-free form of investment when compared to other options. You must ensure that your funds can be easily accessed when needed as if not, it defeats the purpose of creating an emergency fund. Even if you have tens of thousands of dollars saved away as an emergency fund, what good will it do if you cannot access them?

Sticking to your plan

Once you create your plan, you must follow it. Allow

provisions for a couple of deviations, but not too many. A tricky part of creating an emergency fund is that saving money isn't a simple task. If the goals that you set are attainable, then it becomes easier to follow your plan. An excellent way to do this is by automating the process of saving funds. You can set up an automatic system of transfer of specific sum form your savings account or checking account and get it transferred to another account for safekeeping. Also, please ensure that the funds you save for an emergency don't get mixed up with any other savings or investments you want to make.

Once you have attained your goal for creating an emergency fund, the next step is to use any extra cash you have towards repaying your debts, if you have any. You can use those extra funds for investing or even add them to your savings for retirement. Now that you are aware of the different steps that have been enumerated in this chapter along with the other factors, which you must consider while setting up an emergency fund, the next step is to start planning it all out.

CHAPTER FIVE

RISK-FREE INVESTMENT

You are free to invest in more than one type of instrument and you certainly don't have to restrict yourself. One way in which you can reduce volatility is by diversification of assets or investments. You can include a couple of alternative assets like commodities along with risk-free and low-risk investments to mitigate the risk of loss. By including commodities to your portfolio, you can easily counteract the effects of inflation on your investments. Well, even when the price of other investments like stocks or mutual funds decreases during inflation, the price of commodities tends to shoot up. If you aren't keen on taking any risks or have limited risk tolerance, then you must invest in an instrument when the market is stable. It is all about trying to earn a profit even when the market seems bearish or bullish. Even when the value of your investments, like real estate, antiques, and other valuables hasn't been updated in the quarterly brokerage statement, you must know the value of your investment portfolio. Even if such items aren't sold off easily, their value and associated risks needs to be taken into consideration before you consider expanding your portfolio.

There are a couple of things that you must never do while you are designing and assembling your investment portfolio. Most of the investors tend to make certain mistakes that you must avoid. You must ensure that your investment decision is not based on a market fad. Don't follow any random fads that crop up. Instead, your investment decisions must always be based on thorough research and understanding of the financial markets along with the instruments. You cannot have a "set it and forget it" mentality when it comes to investing. You must review your investment portfolio and make changes as needed. You must diversify and change your pattern of asset allocation to mitigate the risk on investment. It takes a long time to make up for any setback that your portfolio might have encountered. So, be thorough in your research before you decide about investing.

Bank Savings

A savings account generates income on the deposits that you hold at the bank or any other financial institution. The interest rates offered aren't too high and are quite modest. Financial institutions often offer such savings account, which limits the number of withdrawals that can be made. They might also levy a certain fee unless a specific minimum balance is maintained in the account.

So, how does this work?

A savings account is usually opened to save such money that doesn't have any immediate or daily expenses. A savings account is quite different from a checking account. As the name suggests, a checking account makes provision for using checks along with any electronic means of debt for accessing the funds. Also, savings account tends to limit the number of withdrawals or the transactions to be made by the account holder every month, and this might not be necessarily applicable to a checking account.

How can a savings account help you?

The importance of maintaining a savings account cannot be overlooked. It helps you set some money aside for your financial needs. You can use this account to save funds you need for holidays, college tuitions, or even a wedding. Other expenses that you can pay for with your savings are purchasing any real estate or a car perhaps. However, there are other means to pay for these, and holding a savings account is merely one option available. In this section, you will learn about the different benefits of using a savings account as a means of investment.

A savings account is an interest-based account wherein interest gets accrued over a period. Please don't be under any misconceptions that opening a savings account is similar to maintaining a piggybank. When you place some money in the piggy bank, the funds neither increase nor decrease and stay the same. However, when you deposit money in a bank, then your account gets credited with a certain amount as interest every year. So, you can substantially increase your finances, while making sure that there are no risks involved. Opening a savings account is believed to be one of the safest methods of investment.

You can certainly reach for your credit card whenever you lack any money and might look for other means to fund your needs, instead of spending money that you didn't have and then worrying about increasing your debt. You must start controlling your use of credit cards. A credit card will not do you much good if you get stuck in a rather unfortunate situation. For instance, if you lose your job, how can you cover all your basic needs using a credit card? Surely you can make do until your credit limit is exhausted, but then again you will need to think about the repayment as well.

Another great thing about the modern banking system is that your funds are available and can be accessed at any point in time. You don't have to worry about time zones or boundaries.

However, on the downside, the rate of interest offered by banks on a savings account is quite low when compared to any other form of investment. Apart from this, there are several restrictions placed on the number of withdrawals you can make along with a minimum balance you must maintain.

Zero Coupon Bonds

Zero coupon bonds are basic bonds that follow extremely simple rules. Here, there are no complications, and everything is straightforward. Now, say for example you buy bonds worth $400 today that have an expiry date five years from now. Once they reach their maturity period, these bonds will be worth $800 each. So, for a period of five years, you will receive a consistent rate of interest for your investment. These are extremely safe choices for you, and the rate of interest is also higher than what your federal government or agency will pay.

Here, the bond that you receive today will actually be worth $800. However, you will get it at a big discount now and then cash it in, in full, after a certain amount of time. Don't think of this as a bad scheme, as your money will be safe, and you will have the chance to double what you have in due course.

It is, however, not comparable to stocks, as it might not take so long to receive a return on your investment. Bonds are safer options for you, but you will not be able to invite large returns from these types of investments.

There are many situations where people can use zero coupon bonds. A basic example is a parent saving money for his or her child's college fund. It is easy to invest money that will mature by the time a child is college age. This will help pay for the cost of college. Another example is wealthy people using zero coupon bonds to leave as an inheritance for family members. These beneficiaries do not have to pay as much tax as they would if it was not a bond. Sometimes zero-coupon bonds are tax exempt, especially those issued by a government agency while those issued by a corporation are not tax exempt. For these kinds of bonds, you will have to pay income tax for earning that you have not yet received.

Government Bonds

Government bonds are those that are issued by the government. This means that these bonds are securities that the government of your country will issue for you. Government bonds can be issued by both the central and the state government. These bonds are money that the government borrows from the public. The government needs this money to carry out their various businesses, including construction, renovation, repair, etc. Although the government will already have some money, it cannot operate on that money alone.

These types of bonds have existed for a long time, and the government has issued millions of bonds to date. That makes for a debt of nearly 20 trillion dollars owing to all the bonds that have been issued to date. Here, you must understand that the government will collect taxes from citizens and try to recover the money for the bonds. However, the amount collected will often be insufficient, and several bonds will have reached maturity date. Now, they cannot turn away the people that they have not paid as yet, and they must ensure that everybody gets their money. Under such a circumstance, they will borrow this money and pay off their bondholders. Doing this for a long time can cause the economy of a country to destabilize. This destabilization can affect those who invest in stocks, as people are not going to spend as much during an economic crisis, no matter how big or small it seems.

However, from an investor's point of view, this is a good investment as there is minimal credit risk at play. This means that there is no real danger of the investor not getting his or her money back in full. Thus, government bonds make for the right choice for all those looking for a safe option to invest in. However, you must remember that your credit risk needs to be high if you wish to make the most of your investment.

"High risk, high reward" is the ultimate anthem of the stock market, and with bonds, that is not a possibility. Although there will be the danger of you losing half or all your money in credit risk investments, the possibility of doubling or even tripling is high. This makes it a worthwhile investment for you because you don't have to worry about suffering any losses.

There are different types of government bonds that you can choose from. Each one comes with its own set of advantages, and you have to choose the one that suits your investment type the best. Many brokers these days will advise you against investing in these bonds, as the American debt level is consistently rising. However, the ultimate choice lies with you alone, and you will have to decide for yourself whether you want to invest in government bonds!

The type of bond you can buy from the government is dependent on the bond's maturity. Short-term bonds are called bills, and they mature in less than a year. Notes are the medium-term bonds that mature between one and ten years. While bonds themselves are the long-term ones, who take more than ten years to mature, these bonds are better known as treasury bonds or treasury bills.

Certificate of Deposit

A certificate of deposit or a CD is essentially a savings certificate that has a fixed date of maturity along with a fixed interest payable to its holder. If you invest your funds in a CD, then your access to those funds is restricted until the instrument reaches its maturity. These instruments are usually issued by commercial banks and the Federal Deposit Insurance Corporation or FDIC insures them for up to the amount of $250,000 per investor.

A bank usually issues CDs that are promissory notes. It is a time-bound deposit, which restricts its holder from withdrawing the funds as and when they please. It is usually issued in electronic form and can also be automatically renewed upon its maturation. Whenever a CD matures, then the holder of the CD can withdraw the principal along with all the accrued interest. No additional fees are chargeable on a CD if they are withdrawn before they mature. The interest rates offered by most CDs happen to be higher than the one offered by savings accounts.

CDs are based on the idea that you can get a higher return by giving up liquidity for the time being. Under usual market conditions, the interest rates on long-term CDs is slightly higher than the ones offered on short-term CDs. The rate of return provided by CDs isn't exceptionally high and is certainly not more than the returns that you can get from stocks or other high-risk investments. The good thing about investing in CDs is that your funds are secured until their maturity. Not only are they secure, but you will also earn interest on them. If you make an early withdrawal from a CD, then you are liable to pay an early withdrawal penalty and this amount depend on the duration of the CD along with the institution issuing it. Early withdrawal penalties are usually equivalent to the interest payable.

CDs are usually non-negotiable. Simply put, it means that the instrument cannot be transferred, exchanged, or even sold.

Usually, a non-negotiable CD is eligible for an early withdrawal prior to its maturity provided you pay the early withdrawal fees. On the other hand, negotiable CDs or NCDs are the exact opposite of a non-negotiable CD. NCDs are usually issued for large denominations and tend to have a maturity period between a two-weeks until one year. Any CD issued for less than $100,000 is referred to as small CDs. At times, some CDs might also require a minimum investment. Usually, negotiable CDs can be either small or large CDs.

Money Market Funds

Any type of mutual fund which primarily invests in instruments that with a high liquidity like cash, cash equivalents, or any other securities with a high credit rating with a short-term maturity are referred to as money market funds. The liquidity offered by these funds is quite high whereas the associated risks are almost negligible. Money market funds are also referred to as money market mutual funds and function like any other regular mutual fund. They are issued in the form of redeemable instruments or shares to the interested individuals and the must be in compliance with all the rules and regulations given by the United States Securities and Exchange Commission.

A money market fund can invest in any type of debt-backed financial instrument like certificates of deposits, commercial paper, banker's acceptance, treasury bills, as well as any other repurchase agreements.

Investment in Dividend Shares

Most people tend to invest in dividend-based stocks to take advantage of the endless benefits they promise, as well as the reinvestment opportunities they offer to buy additional stock. The majority of the dividend-bearing shares are companies that are generally considered to be financially sustainable, and there is a possibility that dividends will increase steadily over some time. In the meantime, the shareholder may receive regular distributions in the form of dividends. For example, a company may receive a dividend of 205% for one year and increase it to 3% next year. However, this cannot be said with certainty. As soon as the company gains a reputation for reliable dividends that will increase over time, it will strive not to disappoint its investors.

A company that can pay steadily increasing dividends is financially stable and generates sufficient cash flow (as dividends are declared from revenues). Such companies are considered stable, and their share prices are not as volatile as other companies. Dividend-paying stocks are considered to be less risky and therefore more attractive to young investors looking for long-term returns as well as to retirees or retirees. This is a good source of income. The ratio between the stock price and the dividend yield also strengthens investor confidence. When share prices fall, earnings per share increase.

Warrants

A warrant is similar to an option. The holder has the right and not an obligation for buying the underlying security at a specified price and quantity at some time in the future. An option is an instrument that is traded on the stock exchange, whereas a company will issue a warrant. The security that is represented by the warrant, usually an equity share, will be delivered by the company issuing it instead of the investor holding those shares. Companies usually include warrants as a part of their new issue offering. This is offered for attracting investors and also for improving the confidence of a shareholder in the stock. This is conditional to an actual increase in the value of the underlying security over a while. A warrant is a kind of equity derivative.

For instance, shares of a company have a market value of $1.50 per share. You will need to invest $1500 to purchase 1000 shares. However, if the investor opted to invest in warrants (where one warrant represents one share) that were priced at $.50 per warrant, then such an investor would be in the ultimate possession of 3000 shares for the same investment. The leverage and the gearing that is offered by warrants tends to be high due to their low price. This will mean that the potential for reaping capital gains will be more significant. It is quite common that the warrant and share price might be moving in a parallel fashion. However, the proportion of likely gain or loss will differ significantly due to the fundamental difference in their pricing. Another illustration will help you to gain a better understanding of this concept. For instance, the share of a company records a gain of $.30 per share from the initial price of $1.50, it will be $1.80. This shows a 20% gain. However, if the price of a warrant goes from $.30 to $.80, this will indicate a 60% hike. In the given situation, the gearing factor is arrived at by dividing the initial price of the share by the initial price of the warrant ($1.50/$.50 = 3). The gearing factor in this case is 3, and it shows the financial leverage offered by the warrant. The greater this number is, the higher is the potential for profits or losses.

When the market is bullish, the gains offered by warrants are quite significant. They also provide the investor with protection during a bearish market. As the price of the underlying shares drops, the warrants wouldn't probably realize the same loss as compared to the underlying shares. This financial leverage that's offered comes in quite handy.

The leverage that's offered by this instrument is often high. However, this can work to the investor's disadvantage as well. Let us take into consideration the example that was mentioned above. If you have realized a drop by $.30, then the percentage of loss on the share will be 20%, and that incurred on a warrant will be 60%. An increase is always favorable. However, a drop in the same price can prove to be a more considerable disadvantage. The next risk that the investor will face will be that the value of a warrant certificate can plummet to zero as well. If this happens before the rights were to be exercised, then the warrant wouldn't have any redemption value. A warrant doesn't carry any voting rights. The investor won't have a say in any matters regarding the functioning of the company, though their rights will be affected by the company's decision.

CHAPTER SIX

LOW-RISK INVESTMENT

Corporate Bonds

When it comes to investments, you do not have to invest only in equities, but can also invest in debt instruments. You, as an investor, can choose the asset class that you want to invest in based on your risk tolerance. There are different categories of debt instruments. This section provides some information on one category of debt fund schemes known as corporate bond funds.

Corporate Bond Debt Funds

A corporate bond debt fund or a non-convertible debenture can be issued by any company. Companies that want to expand their business or improve their daily operations can use these funds to raise capital for the company. Companies can choose to raise funds through debt or equity investments. Since debt does not affect a shareholder directly, most companies choose to invest in debt funds. It is for this reason that most companies go in for debt. A corporate bond debt fund gives a company an economic way to raise funds when compared to opting for a bank loan.

A corporate bond security is the foundation for any credit opportunity for a debt fund. When you purchase a debt fund, you are loaning the company some money. The firm will only repay the loan amount at the end of the term and will give you an interest amount every month. This interest amount is called the coupon.

Who must invest in a Corporate Bond?

A corporate bond is a good investment choice for you if you are looking for a higher but fixed income from a safe investment option. This investment instrument is a low-risk investment vehicle, and it also ensures some capital protection. If you want to choose a corporate bond fund that puts your money in a high-quality fund, it will serve your financial goal.

A long-term debt fund is often risky since the interest rate will fluctuate beyond the expectations. A corporate bond will always invest in scraps, which will reduce the volatility of the bond. Most corporate bonds can only have a maturity date between one and four years. This is an added benefit if you choose to invest in the bond for more than three years. You can also use this investment to help you be more tax efficient.

Benefits and Features of a Corporate Bond

Components of a Corporate Bond

A corporate bond fund will always invest in a debt paper. Most companies issue a debt paper that includes debentures, bonds, structured obligations and commercial papers. The components listed in the debt paper will carry a maturity date and will also carry a unique risk profile.

Price of the Bond

It is important to remember that no bond is static, and that it always has a price. The price of the bond will change depending on when you choose to purchase the bond. You must always see how the value of the bond varies from the par value, and this difference will explain the par value of the bond.

Par Value of the Bond

The par value of the bond is the amount of money that the issuer of the bond, mostly the company, will give you when the bond matures. This is basically the principal amount. The par value of the bond is usually $100.

Coupon

When you purchase a corporate bond, the company will pay you a regular interest until you sell the bond, or the bond matures. This interest amount is called the coupon amount and is calculated as a percentage of the par value.

Current Yield

The current yield is defined as the annual return that you will make from the corporate bond. For instance, if you own a bond that has a par value of $100, and the rate of the bond is 20%, you will receive an interest of $20 every year from that bond.

Yield to Maturity

The yield to maturity is the in-house rate of return that the company receives for every cash flow associated with the bond. You will receive higher returns when the yield to maturity is greater, and vice versa.

Tax Efficiency

You will need to pay a capital gains tax if you choose to hold the corporate bond for a period less than three years. The amount of tax you will be paying is dependent on your income. If you choose to invest in a long-term investment, you will not have to pay a higher tax.

Allocation and Exposure

Most corporate bond funds are exposed to a government security as well, but this is only done if there is no opportunity available to issue the bond in the credit space.

Risk Factors and Returns

There is a possibility that a bond issuer will default on its obligations. If the company issuing the bond has a lower rate, the possibility of default is higher. Additionally, as the maturity increases, the risk also increases. The risk is minimal when it comes to those companies that have a higher rating. If your fund manager only invests in companies with a higher rating, you can only gain an average return between eight and ten percent. That being said, it is a good idea to invest in a bond issued by a company that has a low rate. For example, a company with bonds that give a higher coupon rate will always attract more investors. There is also the chance that your call or your fund manager's call will go wrong. It is because of this that the corporate bond can be a setback for an investor if the company chooses to default on its interest payments or the rate of the company goes down further.

How Do Corporate Bonds Make Returns?

A mutual fund is much like a fixed deposit, in the sense that it also invests in tradable bonds. Like the share market, there is also a debt market that allows you to trade with numerous bonds. The price of the bonds will fluctuate in this market in the same way that the prices of the shares fluctuate in the share market. For example, if any bond is purchased by a mutual fund, the price of that bond will increase. The bond can then make additional money. This money is more money when compared to the interest of the bond alone. This can also be the other way around.

Types of Corporate Bonds

There are two types of corporate bonds that you can invest in.

Type One

Only high-rated companies like banks and public sector units (PSU) can issue a type one corporate bond.

Type Two

Companies that are rated slightly lower, that is an AA rating or below, can issue type two corporate bonds.

Let us look at the following example to better understand this concept. Suppose, a company that is rated A has a bond that has a default percentage of 0.56% and a one-year residual maturity, while another company rated A has a bond that has a default percentage of 4.79% and a three-year residual maturity. Corporate Bond funds often use the bonds issued by the companies with AA rank or lower in most of their portfolios. It is for this reason that there is a risk that some of the bonds will default, which will result in an impact on the returns from the portfolio.

Points to Remember

There are some points you must remember before you choose to invest in a corporate bond fund.

1. Every corporate bond fund will always invest in different corporate bonds or debentures of long or medium tenure. So, it is important that you look at this type of investment as a long-term investment vehicle.

2. It is important that you have some knowledge about the market in this instance. If you are not someone who has invested in debt funds before, you will find it difficult to understand the market and the risks.

3. You must always look at the past-year returns for a corporate bond before you invest in it. That being said, you must never let it sway you because a large number of defaults within the profile will lead to a drag in the returns.

4. You must always stick to large AMCs when you choose the corporate bond you want to invest in. Always make a list of the top five AMC funds, and

only invest in those. If you do not invest in these, you must stick to another high-rated short-term debt fund where you have a lower credit risk.

Preferred Stocks

A preferred stock, also known as a preference share or preferred share is a security that will represent the ownership that a shareholder has in a corporation. These shareholders will have a priority claim over some common shares in the company's assets and earnings. A preferred share has a higher priority when compared to an ordinary share but is not as important as a bond when compared to other assets. A shareholder with preference shares has a higher priority when compared to those who hold common shares or stocks.

Features of Preferred Shares

A preferred share has many features that are a combination of both a common equity and debt. The terms of the investments may vary, but there are some common features:

Preference in Assets upon Liquidation

A preferred share gives every shareholder more priority when compared to a common shareholder, especially when the company is about to be liquidated.

Dividend Payments

Every share will give the shareholder a dividend payment, and the payments can either be floating or fixed. This is dependent on a rate benchmark that is provided by LIBOR.

Preference in Dividends

Every preferred shareholder will have some priority over a common shareholder when it comes to the dividend payments.

Non-Voting

Most shares do not give their shareholders their own voting rights. That being said, some of preference shareholders are given additional rights when it comes to their votes.

Convertibility to Common Stock

You can convert a preferred share into a common share depending on the agreement. There are some preference shares that will specify the dates on which these shares need to be converted. That being said, there are some shares for which there must be an approval provided by the board of directors.

Callability

Every share can be repurchased by the issuer on some dates depending on what is agreed upon between the issuer and the shareholder.

Types of Preferred Stocks

Preferred stocks are the perfect type of investment that you as an investor can make. There are different types of preferred stocks.

Convertible Preferred Stock

A convertible preferred share can always be converted into an ordinary share. The management can determine the number of ordinary or common shares the investor can convert the preferred stock into.

Cumulative Preferred Stock

If the issuer does not pay the dividend on the said date, the amount will be added to the next payment.

Exchangeable Preferred Stock

The investor can choose to exchange a preferred share for any other type of security.

Perpetual Preferred Stock

There is no guarantee when the shareholder can receive the capital.

Advantages of Preferred Shares

Both the holders and the issuers of a preferred share will benefit from it. An issuer may be benefitted in the following ways through preferred shares:

No Dilution of Control

This type of financing will allow an issuer to either defer or avoid the dilution of control, as the shareholders do not have the right to vote when they own these instruments.

No Obligation for Dividends

The issuer of the share is not obligated to pay any dividend to the shareholder. This means that the company can choose to avoid paying a dividend if it does not have the necessary funds to make the payment.

Flexibility of Terms

The terms for any preferred share can be discussed and agreed upon by the management or board of the company.

A preferred share is an attractive alternative investment for most investors. You as an investor can be benefited in the following ways:

A Secure Position in Case the Company Is Liquidated

Every investor who has a preferred share is always in a better condition when compared to an investor who only owns common shares. These shareholders have a priority in claiming the assets of the company.

Fixed Income

Most companies can and are willing to pay their shareholders a dividend every year. They are always willing to pay the shareholder a fixed income.

Annuities

An annuity is a great investment to consider if you wish to earn a steady income during your retirement. You must understand what the different types of annuities are and how they work. This chapter will shed some light on different annuities. You must use this information to help you choose the right annuity for your retirement portfolio.

The Big Picture

There are many investors who are willing to invest in long-term investments, but there are a few investors who are willing to invest in short-term investments. The latter do not mind watching their investments rise and fall on a regular basis. There are some investors, especially those who are nearing their retirement age, who cannot accept any short-term volatility in their portfolios. If you are an investor who has a moderate or low risk tolerance, you must choose to invest in an annuity.

Points to Remember

Investors usually acquire annuities to create a steady stream of income for themselves during their retirement. The two major types of annuities you must consider are immediate and deferred annuities. The tax benefits offered by annuities include tax-deferred growth, but the amount you withdraw will be added to your income for the calculating your income tax. Most annuities levy a penalty on early withdrawals. The contract of annuity is formed between the insurance company and the annuitant or the investor. The insurance company offers to pay a specific sum of money for a specific period.

Tax Benefits of Annuities

There are many tax benefits offered by an annuity. The earnings help you avoid paying out too much tax, especially during the accumulation phase of the annuity contract. You will only need to pay an income tax when you begin to withdraw money from the annuity.

If you use an IRA to contribute to the annuity, or any other tax-advantaged retirement account to transfer money to the annuity, you will be able to decrease your taxable income. This will help you save your contribution to the tax. Your tax savings will compound over a period of time and will help to boost your returns.

Additionally, you will not be able to predict when you will die. It is for this reason that the insurance company is only worried about your average retirement lifespan. It is very easy for the insurance company to predict the average lifespan of the clients. The insurer will only operate on certainty. It is for this reason that the insurance company will price the annuity marginally to ensure that it will retain more money when compared to the amount that it will need to payout to the clients. The client will still receive a certain income from the insurance company.

An annuity offers investors numerous provisions like a guaranteed number of years when payments will be made. If you, as the investor, die before the amounts are paid, the insurer will either pay the amount to the spouse, partner or the estate. The monthly payments will be smaller if the number of guarantees increase in the contract.

Issues to Consider

When it comes to an overall retirement plan, it does make sense to include an annuity. Before you purchase an annuity, you must consider the following:

Are you only planning to invest in an annuity for a long- term goal or are you saving for your retirement? Are you choosing to invest in the annuity because you are looking for a tax-advantaged plan? If the answer to that is yes, you must realize that you will not be gaining any additional benefit?

When it comes to a variable annuity, will you be okay if the value of the account fell to a value that is below the amount that you had initially invested because the fund or the portfolio you invested in did not do well? Are you aware of the expenses and fees you will incur when you choose to invest in an annuity? Do you wish to hold the annuity for a long period so you can avoid paying any surrender charges when you choose to withdraw the money from the account? If you do withdraw money from the annuity, are you aware of how it will affect your tax liability?

The Bottom Line

An annuity offers a growth that is tax deferred. This can result in a long-term return that will be significant. You must always contribute to the annuity for a lengthy period and only withdraw these funds once you retire. The tax benefits offered by a deferred annuity will always amount to substantial savings, and you will be at peace. You must always understand what you will gain from an annuity before you add it to your retirement profile.

CHAPTER SEVEN

HIGH-RISKINVESTMENT

If the type of investment you want to invest in offers a high rate of return within a short duration, it usually means that the investment is somewhat risky. With the right time, most of the investments can help double the principal of yourinvestment. However, a lot of investors tend to opt for high-yield investments that expire within a short period even though the probability of risk on such investments is quite high. Please remember that there is no scientific formula you can follow to double your investment using any instrument. However, there are several instances wherein investments doubled in value within a short period. For every one of those investments that turned out exceptionally well, there are hundreds of investments that didn't go as planned. So, the burden of ensuring that you choose the right instrument rests on your shoulders.

There is a simple technique known as the rule of 72, which can be used for determining the time it will take for an investment to double given that its rate of interest stays fixed. When you divide the annual rate of return by 72, it will give you a rough estimate of how long it will take for the initial investment to at least double itself. For instance, if you are investing a dollar with an interest rate of 10% per annum, then it will take 7.2 years for the dollar to double itself (72 years/10= 7.2 years). So, if you have the time and patience, then you can use this rule to double your money.

Invest in Options

Options certainly offer a high rate of return on investment. When you purchase an option, you have an offer to purchase an underlying stock or commodity at a given price at a specific time in the future. If the price of the security increases during its maturity, then you can decide to purchase or sell the security. However, if the value of the commodities doesn't increase as desired, the investor doesn't have to purchase the securities. This is quite a risky form of investment because the purchase or the sale of securities needs to be finalized within a specific period.

The advantage of investing in an option is that you are given the chance of acquiring stocks at a nominal value and then wait for their value to increase before paying for them in full. If the value of the option doesn't increase, then you lose the advance you put down, and nothing more than that. It is a high-risk investment, and therefore the returns on it are high as well. When done correctly, an investor can acquire this instrument for a low price and sell it when the price increases for earning a profit. Options are quite flexible and can work well with any method of trading.

The disadvantage of this instrument is that the stock prices don't usually fluctuate drastically, whereas the value of options does. If speculation isn't your forte, then you must stay away from options. These investments are risk capital investments, and this means that the capital you invest in this instrument is risky, and it can swing either way for you. You might get the opportunity to earn a profit or even lose your capital. Once the period lapses, the option expires, and it becomes worthless.

Securitization

Securitization is the process of creating a financial instrument by combining different financial assets and then marketing these different tiers of securities to investors, and this process can comprise of different types of financial assets, and it also helps to promote liquidity in the market. Securities that are backed by mortgage will be a perfect instance of securitization. By clubbing up the mortgages, the issuer can then divide this huge pool into smaller parts based on the risk of default of each of these individual mortgages and then resell these smaller portions to the investors.

This process helps to create liquidity by letting the smaller investors acquire shares that form a part of the more prominent asset pool. Making use of mortgage-backed securities, the individual investor can purchase a part of the mortgage as a kind of bond. Without securitization, the individual investor might not be able to afford to buy into the bigger pool of mortgages present. The company that is holding the loans is referred to as the originator, and they will gather the necessary data on different assets that it will take out from their related balance sheets. These assets will then be gathered together based on factors like the period remaining on loan, the risk involved, and so on. This group of assets that have been gathered together will then be sold to an issuer. The issuer will then create a set of tradable securities representing a stake in the associated assets and will, in turn, sell the same to investors who are interested at a special rate.

Securitization will provide the creditors with a means of lowering the associated risks through the dissection of the ownership of the obligations of debt. The investors will assume the position of a lender by purchasing the security. The investor can earn a return that is based on the principle of association and the payments towards interests that are made by the debtors under their obligation. Unlike other forms of investments, this particular type of investment is based on tangible goods. In case of a default in payment by the debtor, then the underlying asset can be seized and sold for compensating for the default in payment. Like with any other investment, the higher the risk involved, the higher will be the potential of returns on it.

Exchange-Traded Commodity or ETCs

Exchange traded commodities are referred to as ETCs, and they give the trader and the investor exposure to commodities via shares. These are traded like a stock, which is they are traded on a stock exchange. ETCs track the movement of the price of the underlying commodity like oil, silver and even gold and their prices will fluctuate depending on the value of these underlying commodities. ETCs can track individual commodities or even a basket of commodities. For instance, an ETC basket will be an instrument that will track multiple metals instead of one or it can even track different agricultural commodities like wheat, soybeans, and corn. The structure of the ETCs can vary depending on the issuing company. There are individual exchanges around the world like the London stock exchange and the Australian Securities Exchange that will offer ETCs with a specific structure. These ETCs will track the price of the commodity. There will be a management fee that will be charged, and this will be the compensation for the company that's running these instruments. ETCs will provide a net asset value, and this is the fair value of an ETC. The commodity market can be a physical or a virtual marketplace for trading in the commodities. There are about 50 commodity markets that are present around the world, and there are about 100 commodities that are traded on them. The commodities can be categorized as hard and soft commodities. Natural resources that can be mined or extracted like gold, rubber, and oil will be examples of hard commodities. Soft commodities, on the other hand, will be agricultural products or even livestock like corn, wheat, pork, and so on.

There are different ways in which you can invest in commodities. The stock can be purchased in those corporations whose business is dependent on commodity prices or even invest in mutual funds or ETFs that focus on companies related to commodities. The direct way of investing in these investments will be by buying a futures contract. A future contract will place an obligation of buying or selling the commodity at a specific price on the date of delivery sometime in the future. The major commodity exchanges in the US are located in Chicago and New York.

Hedge Fund

A hedge fund is an alternative type of investment that pools together the capital obtained from different individual or institutional investors and invests that capital in different assets to build a diverse portfolio and effectively manage the risks. Hedge funds tend to invest in various types of varied investments ranging from real estate, to commodities, and to available alternative assets. This is one of the primary differences between a hedge fund and a mutual fund, which normally restricts its investments to stocks or bonds. The goal of a hedge fund is to maximize the returns to an investor while reducing and hedging the risk regardless of whether the market's health is up or down. Hedge funds became rather popular during the streak of bullish markets in the US economy in the 1920's before the great depression. At present, hedge funds are valued at several trillions of dollars.

Hedge funds are usually perceived to be quite an aggressive and risky form of investment, especially when compared with the more conservative options available in the market. The investment strategy followed differs from one hedge fund to another, but the idea of all the hedge funds is the same- to use trading techniques that help to hedge their bets and prevent any losses to their clients. The success of a hedge fund essentially depends on the ability of the hedge fund manager to anticipate any changes in the market and react in a suitable manner.

Hedge funds tend to invest in a variety of investment options ranging from real estate, to currencies, to alternative assets and everything else in between. Since hedge funds are privately owned, they are free to do as they please with the funds as long as they are being upfront with their clients. This degree of leniency toward the hedge fund manager makes the investment quite risky. Essentially, your chances of earning a profit or incurring a loss are dependent on the hedge fund manager's ability to think and make decisions. However, this does also give this investment a lot of flexibility.

Structured Products

Structured products have been designed for facilitating customized risk-return goals. This is made possible by taking any regular security like the conventional bond and then replacing the usual features of payments with a couple of unconventional payoffs that are derived not from the cash flow of the issuer, but the performance of the underlying assets. The return on these investments will depend on the performance of the underlying assets. If the return on the underlying asset is "x," then the payout on the structured product will be "y." This will mean that the performance of the structured product will be related to the traditional model of option pricing, even though they might contain other types of derivatives like swaps, forwards, and even futures as well as several embedded features like downside buffers. Structured products had become popular in the European markets, and they have gained popularity in the US as well. In the US, they are made available as products registered with the SEC. This means that they will be available to investors in the same manner as stocks, bonds, ETFs, and even mutual funds. These investments can offer customized exposure to usually hard to reach classes and subclasses of assets that will make these structured products a useful component of a diversified portfolio.

Let us look at an example to get a better understanding of how these instruments function. For instance, a big bank has issued these structured products in the form of notes where each of these notes has a face value of $1000. Each note will be a package that will comprise two components like a zero-coupon bond and a call option on the underlying instrument, like the common stock or an ETF that will mimic a popular index like the S&P 500 with a maturity period of three years. The pricing of this instrument will be complex. However, the principle involved is quite simple. On the date of issue, you will have to pay the face value, which is $1000 per note. This will be a principal protected investment, which means you will get the $1000 you have invested on maturity regardless of what will happen to the underlying asset. Now, let us look at the performance aspect of this instrument. Let us assume that the underlying asset happens to be a European call option. The return you will earn will depend on the value of the investment at the date of its maturity. If this happens to be higher than the issuing value, then in such a case, you will earn a profit in addition to the original principal. However, if the option is worthless on the date of expiration, you will receive your original principal without any additions to it. This means you will get your $1000 back on maturity.

In the previous example, the key feature is the protection of the principal. In a different situation, the investor might be willing to trade all or some of this protection offered in favor of a performance feature, which is more attractive. Consider another scenario. The investor wants to trade off the principal protection for a combination of other performance features.

A common risk that all structure products possess will be the lack of liquidity due to the customized nature of these investments. Until the date of the maturity, the full return from this investment cannot be realized. This is the reason because of which the structured products tend to be an investment decision that goes along the lines of "buy and hold." Apart from liquidity, the other risk associated with this form of investment will be the credit quality of the issuer. The cash flow is derived from other sources; the product on its own is considered to be the liability of the financial institution that is issuing it. Also, there is no transparency in pricing strategies.

That is, there is no uniform pricing standard for these investments. This will be difficult for making a comparison of different structured offerings.

Angel Investor

The term angel investor is used to denote a private investor who offers finance and support a business requires during its initial stages. Becoming an angel investor is quite a risky option since you need to have a sense of business acumen along with basic knowledge about the business you want to get involved in. Angel investors are usually offered shares, or any other form of security of the business that represents debt, equity, or a combination of the two. They are also referred to as business angels. In the past, angel investors were often entrepreneurs who exited their business and wanted to help newcomers get a foothold in the industry by mentoring them and helping them raise the necessary capital for their business ventures. Angel investors are usually involved in the business during its conception and inception stages. These are the first outsiders who get effectively involved in a business.

So, what are the different benefits an investor can get? Well, the risk taken by an angel investor is rather significant and high. Therefore, the returns offered on this type of investment are high too. If you are looking for a significant payout, then this is a good option. In some countries, an angel investor is also eligible for certain tax concessions. For instance, in the UK, an angel investor can claim tax reliefs according to the Seed Enterprise Investment Scheme and the Enterprise Investment Scheme. If you have good ideas and are knowledgeable about your chosen niche, then you can always offer advice to the business you invest in. Apart from this, it is a great way to increase your business network and create a name for yourself as an angel investor in the market.

However, there are certain risks associated with becoming an angel investor. The first and the most obvious risk of all is the fact that investing in a startup is a risky gamble. When it comes to startups, the concept of taking calculated risks doesn't exist. Even if the idea sounds lovely to you, there is no guarantee that the startup will be successful. If the business goes into a loss, then your investment can be lost! If you want to become an angel investor, another thing you must consider is the time taken to earn your returns. It might offer high returns, but to earn such high returns, you must stay in the game for longer. A lot of people seem to think that they can exit the game after maybe three to five years, but ideally, you must stay in the game for ten years to earn excellent returns, provided everything goes favorably and as planned.

CONCLUSION

I want to thank you for choosing this book. I hope it proved to be an informative and enjoyable read.

By now, you will have realized that attaining your financial dream is a practical goal. However, to attain that goal, you need some time, effort, and the right resources. Armed with the information given in this book, you can achieve the financial freedom you always desired.

The first step toward attaining your financial goals is to analyze your current financial status, decide your goals, and then make a plan of action to attain those goals. There are different types of investment options you can utilize. According to your financial capacity, the risks involved, and the returns you expect, you need to identify the best possible investment options. Apart from this, you must also consider budgeting and creating an emergency fund to ensure that you always have the finances you need.

Now, all that's left for you to do is get started and the take the first step toward budgeting and investing.

Thank you and all the best!